Mission of love

11/1/2020

To dearest Nikki

Hoping you find as
much peace, love
& happiness in this
book as I did.

With very much love

Cally

♡ ♡ xxx

A physician's
personal
journey
towards a
life beyond

Mission of love

ROGER COLE

Lothian
BOOKS

Thomas C. Lothian Pty Ltd
11 Munro Street, Port Melbourne, Victoria 3207

Copyright © Roger Cole 1999
First published 1999

National Library of Australia
Cataloguing-in-Publication data:

Cole, Roger, 1955– .
  Mission of Love

  ISBN 0 85091 915 0.

  1. Meditation. 2. Self-realization. 3. Spiritual healing.
  4. Death — Psychological aspects. I. Title.

158.1

Design by Page Pty Ltd
Printed in Australia by Griffin Press Pty Limited

Foreword

It has always astonished me how many doctors turn out to be good writers, this especially, after looking at your average prescription one is forced to conclude that most medical practitioners must be verging on the illiterate.

It is perfectly valid to use the defence that content is more important than form, that what we have to say is more important than how we say it. Frankly, Roger Cole's book contains enough good material to make it valid if it had been written in mumble and grunt. But it isn't. It is delightfully written and lovingly told. This is a book we have waited half a century to be written. That is ever since the medical profession became obsessed with pills and potions and forgot about love and caring. It will bring joy, relief, hope and understanding to a great many lives. How I wish it had been available when first we heard that Damon, our youngest son, was going to die of AIDS.

Roger Cole came into our lives when our son Damon was in the final stages of AIDS. He was born a haemophiliac and contracted the HIV virus from a blood transfusion in the very early days of the pandemic. At that time virtually nothing was known about the virus and, putting it into lay terms, the doctors, seemingly willy-nilly, threw everything at it, often with quite disastrous results.

To those readers who do not know the prognosis of AIDS, perhaps a short explanation? In a nutshell, the AIDS virus destroys the T-cells in our body. These are the cells which fight off infection, the infantry troops that prevent most of the deadly viruses and diseases, which lurk at the peripherals of everyone's life, from entering our bodies. In other words, they largely constitute our immune system. The AIDS virus eventually destroys all these T-cells allowing any number of diseases to invade the body without being repulsed.

The AIDS sufferer doesn't in a sense, die from a disease known as AIDS, but from a multiple number of infections which combine to kill him or her. At any stage he or she may be suffering with two or three different viral diseases, all of which require essentially different treatments using drugs which don't always work together. Add to this the fact that Damon was a haemophiliac which in itself required constant and complex medication and the result was that he was taking an uncoordinated cocktail of drugs with disastrous effects.

One such drug would give him acute constipation which, in his weakened state, was severe enough to be life-threatening, the next would bring on diarrhoea which would leave him dangerously dehydrated, a third created acute nausea and yet another caused him to have severe fits. While it may seem curious in today's medical climate, with five different doctors caring for Damon at one time, none of them, to my knowledge, saw fit to check on the treatment each of the others had prescribed.

Damon was quite simply dying of the medication he was receiving and doing it real tough.

Then Roger Cole entered our lives. In my book *April Fool's Day*, there are two sentences which simply read: 'Dr Cole, if you read this book, please know how very much we are in your debt. Damon loved you and we thank you for your honesty, compassion and love.'

Roger Cole soon had Damon on a drug regimen that levelled out the peaks and the valleys, which made his life a great deal more comfortable. AIDS is an awful way to die, simply because you die of everything. All I can say is that, but for Roger Cole, my son would have died a terrible, terrible death. It isn't simply that he is a brilliant palliative care specialist, which he certainly is, but because as a man he returns the somewhat tarnished reputation of the medical profession back into a brilliance that makes him a wonderful exception, not only as a doctor, but as a human being.

Roger Cole, may your book sell a hundred thousand copies just for starters. It is a wonderful complement to your skill as a physician and will, I know, lead many a confused, desperate, weary and grieving family lost in a dark depression back into the pure light of understanding and hope.

Bryce Courtenay

Contents

Acknowledgements

*I*n writing *Mission of Love* I am indebted to the Patients and carers that I have seen as a palliative care physician. You have taught me to look deeper, to find love, to be less judgemental and to be more compassionate.

I have included many case studies in the text. For the majority, confidentiality has been maintained by writing composite stories or by altering details such as names, gender or diagnosis. In some instances identities are revealed or the stories are recognisable. I especially thank those of you who gave permission for their inclusion. You know who you are and I wish you to know that this has meant a great deal to me.

Mission of Love could not have been written without the wisdom of the Brahma Kumaris World Spiritual University. Many of the insights included within it reflect their teaching of Raja Yoga Meditation. I would especially like to thank Baba, Dadi Janki and Didi Nirmala for their spiritual knowledge and guidance during the development of this book. Royalties from the sale of this book are dedicated to the worldwide service of this organisation.

I would also like to thank the people who read and commented on earlier drafts of this manuscript. I am especially grateful to Therese Nichols and Jo Heathcote in this regard.

Last but not least to Sue, Sam and Lucinda, my wholehearted love and gratitude for the time I didn't spend with you.

Preface

I have been a doctor since 1979 and don't recall ever wanting to be anything else. I can't honestly say that compassion was my driving force. On the contrary, I was a high achiever ambitious for success and recognition, driven by self-interest and a fear of failure. There was nothing in my undergraduate training at Guy's and King's College Hospitals in London to change this. I was trained to be scientific, clinically detached and uninvolved with human suffering. I left university without knowing that people need doctors who communicate and care. Actually, caring embarrassed me. It made me feel vulnerable.

In my final year as a medical student I did a six-week paediatric term in Darwin and fell in love with Australia. On an impulse I arranged to return to Darwin Hospital as an intern after passing the final medical examinations. My wife Sue had just graduated in dentistry and supported the adventure. We had a wonderful year and Sue would have liked to stay but I had ambitions. I wanted to become a specialist physician, which meant a move to Sydney's Royal Prince Alfred Hospital (RPA). I thrived in the competitive, academic environment, which enabled me to remain goal-oriented, self-centred and successful.

By the end of 1983 my greatest moment was passing the physician's specialist examination. This enabled me to enter specialist training in medical oncology (cancer medicine) with no more examinations to face. With three years of further supervision I would become a Fellow of the Royal Australasian College of Physicians (FRACP).

After three months of euphoria I came to earth. Having satisfied my highest aim there was nothing left to strive for. I wasn't focused and I was burning out. There was a lack of discipline in my life and I had an identity crisis. Without a goal I felt empty and didn't know myself. I struggled and looked for new mountains to climb.

Fellow high achievers advised me to publish scientific papers, do research and get a PhD to succeed in medicine. As I thought about this I discovered a new voice inside me. It was saying, 'No. Consider others.' My ambitions had blinkered me into looking on sick people as problems to solve, rather than opportunities to help and to heal. I began to see beyond this arrogance. People didn't get cancer to further my career; they were suffering and so were their families. I needed to understand this better and felt angry towards an establishment which seemed academic and out of touch. I started talking to my patients. I explored what it was like to live with cancer, to face death and to lose someone you love. To my amazement it really helped them and I found people were appreciating me in a way I had never experienced before. They were teaching me to love.

The turning point of my life was a relationship with a young cancer patient who gave me information about a workshop with Elisabeth Kübler-Ross in 1984. Its aim was to help professional people become more effective in caring for the dying. The method, which wasn't disclosed in the advertisement, was to have participants confront emotional pain and repression in a cathartic manner. During the workshop I had a cathartic experience of grief followed by an intense feeling of pure, unconditional love, which is described in Chapter 4. At the same time I felt separated from my physical body and experienced a blissful, unworldly happiness. For the first time in my life I realised that I was a spirit and that love, peace and happiness were natural attributes of the soul. When we suppress these attributes we develop sorrow and disease. I also realised that nobody dies, and that we all eventually rediscover our purity, love and power.

I took the following year out of mainstream oncology to develop a centre at RPA, which provided information, counselling and support for people with cancer. I learnt counselling techniques, developed cancer support groups and researched complementary therapies. I began to meditate and to teach meditation to interested cancer patients and their families. Above all I let down my guard, developed a more open, easy nature and enjoyed being myself in therapeutic relationships. Having found love I now discovered that healing is a balance between competency and compassion. Patients benefited most from my knowledge, skills and understanding when I was simply being myself.

While developing as a physician I also started to integrate spiritual awareness into my work with people suffering from cancer; not by preaching but through the virtues of love and respect. I began to realise that we can reach people through our attitude and nature, and that spiritual development enables us to extend spiritual support without words. Though attracted to leaving medicine and following more esoteric healing practices, an inner voice told me to remain patient and tolerant. I should stay orthodox yet be eccentric to the 'mainstream'. I felt it had been no accident that a spiritual awakening had followed my specialist examination success. I was somehow meant to be where I was. As it is, my colleagues now think of me as 'different' but they respect my judgement. I'm happy with that.

After struggling through my training in oncology I moved into palliative care, becoming the Director of Palliative Care at the Prince Henry and Prince of Wales Hospitals in 1987. Providing comfort, support and relief for people who would die was very rewarding. It seemed such an honest expression of medicine and gave me a sense of serving humanity. There are remarkable lessons to be learnt from caring for people who are dying, especially when the state we call acceptance emerges. A soul is almost visible. Pure and peaceful it can fill a room with love and leave everyone feeling that the 'death' was beautiful. Acceptance reveals an ever-present, though forgotten potential of our souls to love unconditionally.

As I witnessed these things I began to speak of them and found that people were uplifted. It gave them a sense of their spirituality, a feeling of hope and a belief in love. I found in this a sense of vocation. People could awaken or find healing when I shared observations and experiences. It has meant being, at times, both sincere and vulnerable. And at times taking risks within the establishment. This has been rewarding because I now feel love and regard for all those I work with and care for. I have written *Mission of Love* in this vein. It is a composite of stories from my journey with the dying and reflections from my study of meditation.

The aim of this book is to offer knowledge and insight, as well as a route to compassion and peace, in the hope that others will also seek understanding before the end of their lives. The book can best be considered a spiritual tapestry woven from the individual experiences of people's lives, my own included. As spiritual evolution takes us far beyond everyday expression, I have had to search for the right words to express the deepest emotions of my convictions and beliefs.

I begin by relating my approach to people living and

dying with diseases like advanced cancer, AIDS and motor neurone disease. By drawing on personal experiences, and those of my patients, I have depicted spirituality as a process of enlightenment and self-realisation. Several meditation exercises are provided to guide readers through this process and its application to everyday life. Through this, I hope to engage our shared potential for change and growth.

ONE

Dear John...

*J*ohn had AIDS.

Diagnosed four years earlier he had fought a desperate battle to survive through orthodox and complementary medicine. His initial courage and optimism gave way to depression and hopelessness as he sensed failure and faced the inevitability of death. Through love, his partner and family would not give in and encouraged him to keep on fighting. 'With the right attitude, you can still beat it,' they told him. God knows he had tried, he thought.

By the time he was admitted for terminal care, he had suffered. With dark-rimmed eyes in a sunken face, John's body was wasted. Welts oozed from his skin, which was tightly drawn over skeletal features. His ribs protruded beyond painfully thin legs that no longer bore his body-weight.

John was totally dependent. He was also moderately demented and knew he was 'losing' his mind. This misery was compounded by incontinence through AIDS-related diarrhoea. His carers were completely exhausted and requested his admission. John was only twenty-six.

When I met him it was evident that he was close to death. He appeared completely wretched. Yet his eyes were furtive and begged you to go away. I could see it would serve no value to make him tell me his medical history; he needed gentleness, confidence and a sense of human kindness.

1

However he resented my intrusion and I was challenged about how to engage him.

'Does it hurt anywhere?' I asked.

'All over,' he replied. 'Look at me, what do you think!' Angry and confronting, I could feel his resentment. I was confused about how to go on.

'John, I will try to make you more comfortable, and do something about the diarrhoea,' I said. 'I have no idea what it is like to be where you are. I can see you have suffered terribly and I imagine that to be almost unbearable.'

'Almost!' he scoffed. 'Almost! I can't stand it any more.'

'Help me understand it better,' I offered. 'What is so terrible now? What is it that you can't stand any more?' Reluctantly at first but then with animation, he told me about losing his health and with it his dreams and aspirations. He described his physical distress, his black depressions, his anger at those who were 'incompetent' and had failed to heal him. He described his loss of dignity. He told me how he hated counsellors and those who preyed on people like him. Then he went quiet and appeared to withdraw into himself. I decided to take a risk. Rightly or wrongly I asked him, 'Do you believe in any form of after life?'

He surfaced from within himself. Despite being exhausted, his eyes were fierce and their message was clear: 'No bedside conversions,' they said. His words were angry, forceful and very final: 'When you're dead, you're dead. Finished!' In the uncomfortable silence that followed, I felt I had blundered and was at a loss for what to say. I had hoped for a positive 'afterlife' discussion that would have brought him some comfort. Instead it seemed that I had ruined any chance of establishing a trusting relationship. But something occurred to me about the manner of his rejection. I realised that, having suffered for so long, eternal life to John meant eternal suffering. He could only project what he was now experiencing into the future. His hope lay in death because this represented an end to suffering. My introduction of the afterlife, though well meaning, was a direct challenge to this.

I sensed that to give him hope I had to tell him he was dying, and that it would soon be over, even though his family had implored me not to. I said, 'John, you are very near the end. I think there are only a few days remaining. We will make these comfortable for you. There is no need to fight any more. Your suffering will soon be over.' There was a visible change in him. His eyes softened and filled with tears, the shadow of fear lifted. His anger dissolved and he uttered the last two words he ever said to me: 'Thank you.'

There was a visible change in him. His eyes softened and filled with tears, the shadow of fear lifted.

I sat with him as he relaxed, then left the room to see his family. Naturally they were very angry with me for speaking to him of dying but I helped them to understand that I had been sensitive and that it was now better for him to know.

Before John died the following day they had some special time together. Instead of imploring him to keep on fighting they allowed John to die peacefully. In accepting his death, they supported him and let him go.

Before I met John I had already been on a spiritual path for some years. He taught me that spirituality is about sensitivity and responsiveness, rather than form and doctrine. Sensing that his principal need was freedom from suffering, I was able to give him hope. By finding a way to bring peace to his mind, I believe I served a spiritual need. By communicating this to his family, I helped them to let him go. In turn, this allowed him to die peacefully.

In writing this book I am indebted to John. He made me wonder. He made me wonder why some people have to suffer. He made me wonder why we become 'spiritually blind' and separated from our souls. He made me wonder what freedom from fear would be like; how it would be to experience the peace that was evident when he knew he was dying; and whether I would put it off until my own death to find out.

By making me wonder he made me seek understanding.

TWO

Making a Difference

I hung up the phone feeling satisfied that Peter and Wendy were very happy. In less than twenty-four hours their despair had subsided and they were hopeful, which is remarkable considering this was an outcome of palliative care.

On the previous day they had been in my consultation room. At fifty years of age, Peter had incurable secondary spread of cancer to his spine and liver. Ten months earlier, he had undergone surgery to remove the cancer when it was only present in its primary form in the rectum. The operation had been proclaimed a success so they were now very angry with their surgeon. They were also angry with their local doctor who had originally misdiagnosed rectal bleeding as haemorrhoids (piles). Moreover, Peter was in pain and had been told that chemotherapy was of no use in this type of cancer.

As I went over Peter's history with him, I explored his reactions to the critical events. I asked questions like: 'What did you think when you first noticed the bleeding?' and, 'How did you feel when you were told it was cancer?' From the time of his original presentation to the time of diagnosis, there had been a delay of three months, so I also asked whether he had any feelings about this.

When he first noticed the bleeding Peter immediately feared cancer because his father had had 'a terrible death' from the same disease. When the diagnosis was confirmed he was shocked and angry that his doctor hadn't acted more quickly. He and Wendy were full of resentment because they believed that he would have been cured if it had been found earlier. I listened as they expressed their feelings — people need to let go of anger and blame in order to move on with their lives.

When I explored Peter's reaction to the relapse, he told me that it was devastating. Having been reassured by the surgeon, discovering that the cancer had spread was a greater shock than the original diagnosis. He couldn't comprehend how it had happened and felt angry with the surgeon for misleading him.

When he was told that the cancer had spread to his liver, and was given a prognosis of less than six months to live, he felt hopeless and depressed. Peter explained how his father had succumbed, with a painful death, only two months after cancer of the liver had been diagnosed. Peter was also despondent about financial problems and concerned for his wife and adolescent children. Neither Peter nor Wendy knew what to tell the children, and the strain of pretending that all was well had been telling on them. Furthermore they were exhausted from sleepless nights caused by Peter's uncontrolled pain.

By the time I had examined Peter, and was ready to communicate with him, we had a good rapport. Asking him about his experience of the disease had enabled me to understand his feelings and to be aware of his current problems and concerns. In listening to him I had also established how informed he was and had developed an intuitive sense of how to relate to him. It was now important, without giving false hope, to emphasise some positive and hopeful aspects.

I said that although cancer had spread to the liver, there was no immediate threat to his life. He still appeared healthy and the liver was functioning well. I told him that a liver must lose more than seventy per cent of its capacity before the situation would become life-threatening. I explained to him how cancer behaves so that he better understood the disease and how it had spread after surgery.

As it had taken ten months for the secondary cancers to appear, I told Peter that his cancer might not behave too aggressively. I was hopeful that it would be slow-growing and said that the prognosis of 'less than six months' was an average, meaning that many people live longer. I also told him that I had seen some people live for more than two years under such circumstances.

Peter's fear began to recede and he asked me about death and dying. Once the immediacy of death becomes more distant, a patient often finds the courage to table it for discussion. Usually he or she states that it is the process, rather than death itself, which is the main fear. Pain, dependency on others, losing control, and separation from loved ones are the things that distress people the most. As he talked to me about all of these things, Peter relaxed. He was relieved to share the burden. I was able to reassure him that his pain would be controlled, and that very few people die in pain when there is good palliative care. I also told him that complete dependency is rarely protracted in patients with liver secondaries so he would not become bed-bound for months at the end of his life.

I finished the consultation by prescribing pain medications and telling Peter and Wendy that I operate as part of a team. A nurse would visit the following morning and give them a phone contact for after-hours support. We had a social worker who could help them address any practical matters such as financial problems, and who could offer counselling services. Having noted their concerns about the children, I recommended that they keep them informed and say that, although Peter's cancer wasn't going to get better, he was going to stay well for as long as possible. This reflected the current position and I offered to meet the children to help them to better understand the disease.

At the end of the consultation Peter and Wendy said that everything was much clearer and more hopeful. By understanding the disease and their circumstances they were better equipped to deal with the uncertainty of their lives. They could now look ahead and see that there was a future. They also felt supported. Speaking to me the following day, Wendy said that the nurse's visit had given her a feeling of security that she would not be alone.

Palliative care workers make a difference by knowing how to relieve suffering, by meeting information and communication needs, and by extending emotional, social and spiritual support. Through human interest and compassion, palliative care helps patients to move toward the deepest peace, love and understanding accessible to a human being. I am sure of this because so many times I have seen serenity emerge when someone reaches the state of acceptance in the face of imminent death. This may happen in a progressive way or it can occur following a catharsis. Over the next few chapters I will explore the state of acceptance and reflect on its spiritual implications.

By understanding the disease and their circumstances they were better equipped to deal with the uncertainty of their lives.

THREE

Unfinished Business

*I*n the 1970s and 1980s Elisabeth Kübler-Ross made a huge contribution to our understanding of death and dying. As well as writing her landmark book *On Death and Dying* (Touchstone Books, 1997), this Swiss-born American psychiatrist travelled the world, passing on her ideas to health professionals. She taught that love is everyone's potential, that acceptance is integral to love, and that unfinished business separates us from both of these.

Elisabeth identified that acceptance follows a struggle through shock, denial, anger, bargaining and depression, which are all normal reactions to dying. The beauty and peace of complete acceptance is not, however, the average way of leaving this world; many people die while still experiencing any, or all, of these adjustment reactions. It is 'unfinished business' that prevents them from reaching acceptance, although I believe that the process continues after death.

Unfinished business is 'baggage' that we carry from our past, and repressed grief is a major component. Its effect is best seen in the transformation that can follow a catharsis. We will explore this over the next two chapters, and witness a spiritual potential that lies beyond pain, loss and negativity. This potential is accessible to all of us but we must first realise that it exists.

In the early part of my palliative care career, I routinely explored and confronted grief repression. The results were sometimes remarkable but occasionally disastrous. I mention this to caution you about applying the approach that I used with Kristina, as the outcome is uncertain and potentially damaging.

Kristina was a seventy year-old Ukrainian widow. She was admitted to hospital for investigations, which revealed breast cancer with secondary spread to the liver. Although it was incurable she was started on a hormone tablet to control the cancer. Kristina lived alone but had a supportive daughter, two grandchildren and a number of close friends.

Three months later she was readmitted with acute pain in her upper abdomen. Exquisite tenderness over a much larger liver indicated rapid progression of her disease. The pain was easily controlled using morphine and, as she refused to have any further anti-cancer treatment, I was consulted to advise on her continuing care.

Although Kristina's 'acceptance' and her ability to face death were admired, I discovered these to be superficial. Applying a Christian philosophy of the Orthodox Church, she intellectualised that her dying would be 'at the ordained time'. She also told of a 'close relationship' with her family and friends, yet wouldn't discuss her diagnosis with them. When interviewed separately, her daughter revealed that contrary to a 'close relationship', there had been longstanding ambivalence between them. Having never felt loved by her mother, she was now frustrated that Kristina was distancing herself even further. Kristina was discharged to the follow-up of her local doctor, with my services available when needed. Neither Kristina nor her daughter felt that counselling would be helpful.

On review two months later, I found that she had become yellow (jaundiced) from liver failure and was breathless due to fluid on her lung. Her daughter was very distressed and confided that their poor relationship had continued to deteriorate. Her support had been rejected and, unable to embrace or express love for her mother, she felt helpless and inadequate. Kristina had avoided contact with friends and neighbours, isolating herself with an independence that alienated all the people she valued.

Kristina's willingness to discuss and accept death was again impressive. However, it was apparent that she avoided talking about separation or loss. Instead she maintained the strong spiritual framework that safely intellectualised her dying. I decided to probe for grief repression with a question, 'Kristina, have you ever experienced any losses of your own, such as a death in the family?'

She hesitated and showed emotion for the first time during our interviews. With gentle prompting she told of a road accident thirty-five years earlier, in which her six year-old son had been critically injured. He had been admitted to hospital in a coma where Kristina maintained a bedside vigil. She left the hospital for a short period, and when she returned was shocked to find an empty room. During her short time away he had died.

At this point Kristina began to cry, telling me how she had been 'the strong one for the family', suppressing her grief while supporting everyone else. She related how she had never seen the child or said good-bye, how she had missed him all these years, and how guilty she was for allowing him to step onto the road. Kristina broke down, sobbing as she relived the whole experience. No further words were required or possible in the next quarter of an hour, as Kristina let go of the grief she had repressed for so many years. I sat with her the whole time until, gradually, her emotions lightened and she repeated

No further words were required or possible in the next quarter of an hour, as Kristina let go of the grief she had repressed for so many years.

over and over, '… it's better now, it's better now, it's better now'.

Following Kristina's death a month later, her daughter contacted me to express her gratitude. After the catharsis Kristina was loving towards her family, talked openly about her feelings and frequently embraced them. She apologised to her friends, disclosed that she was dying of cancer and finally developed the gentleness and peace of mind that characterise true acceptance.

Grief repression and its resolution affect adaptation to, and acceptance of death. With repressed grief people subconsciously avoid internal pain and sorrow by developing personality traits that counter this vulnerability. Kristina's early responses were self-protective. By intellectualising death she avoided feelings of separation and loss, while her fierce independence, self-isolation and rejection of family shielded her from becoming vulnerable through sympathy and support.

By contrast, following a catharsis of grief and guilt, Kristina fully disclosed her situation and welcomed the support of her family. Beyond her 'unfinished business' we discover that acceptance is a peaceful, open state of mind and not simply an acknowledgement of death. There is deep spiritual significance to the peace that lies beneath the baggage of our lives, and we will explore this further in coming chapters.

As I cautioned before, what I did with Kristina is not always beneficial. Nevertheless, when dying people mention past losses you have their trust and confidence so by listening you can do them good. Let them cry if they need to. You are helping them towards acceptance.

Catharsis: A Personal Experience

I was ten years-old when my sister died.

Elisabeth Kübler-Ross referred to unfinished business as an 'inner pool of pain' that is responsible for all of our negativity and mistrust. She believes that we first have to confront and let go of our own grief before we can effectively care for the dying.

In 1984 my life changed when I 'let go' and discovered the freedom that love brings. It began with Kübler-Ross on one of her Australian teaching tours. I attended a five-day 'Life–Death Transitional Workshop' with ninety other people.

On arrival I was allocated a room to share with a stranger called Phil. I believe it was fate rather than coincidence that had brought us together. He was a burnt-out hospital chaplain, an intensely compassionate soul who was fiercely angry towards the Catholic institution. He perceived it to be unsupportive, impersonal and dissociated from community needs. Mine was a similar position, in albeit different circumstances. I too resented a system that seemed impersonal and uncaring.

At the beginning of the workshop we all assembled in the main auditorium where we spent two hours introducing ourselves. The group, which was comprised of mainly health professionals, also contained psychotherapists, priests, lay people and a few cancer patients. In the second session we were each given a sheet of paper and a set of coloured crayons. Elisabeth asked us to do a drawing to depict our lives at that moment. When completed, Elisabeth selected two drawings from the pile and asked a baffling question. 'Do these two people,' lifting first her right hand then her left for emphasis, 'need to be here?'

Remarkably, she was holding my drawing in her right hand and Phil's in her left. Elisabeth proceeded to discuss the significance of our drawings in relation to repressed feelings. She said that they bore striking similarities. Both were vigorously coloured in red, which signified anger, and generous measures of black, which intimated grief-repression or sorrow. Elisabeth said that our past, present, future and far-distant future are represented in the four quadrants of a page when we draw.

I was impressed by her interpretations and amazed by the coincidental selection of Phil's drawing; I was also happy. Out of a conglomeration of anger and grief, I had drawn a bridge into the top-left corner of the page — my far-distant future. Around the end of it was an abundance of purple, which indicated, we were told, that my life would culminate in spiritual growth.

The next session was very confronting. Elisabeth was sitting at the front of the room between two other facilitators. Before the three of them was a mattress with telephone directories neatly stacked at one end, and a pile of feather-down pillows at the other. On top of the directories was something resembling a truncheon. Viewing the scene I felt puzzled as Elisabeth said to come forward if you needed to express any feelings. There was an expectant silence before a man came forward, knelt on the mattress and did something I was completely unprepared for. He screamed.

I recoiled in shock as Elisabeth placed a telephone directory in front of him, handed him the truncheon and told him to direct his anger. Beating the directory with the truncheon, he first hurled abuse at his father, then at anyone he perceived to have hurt him. Ultimately he finished up in tears for the sorrows he had experienced in his lifetime.

This was the vein of the workshop for the next four and a half days. It was a 'Gestalt' process, dealing with deeply repressed emotions. Ninety 'normal' people went on to share cathartic experiences in an atmosphere that felt increasingly supportive. Elisabeth encouraged us to come forward and express ourselves, when someone or something made us feel vulnerable. Practically every conceivable trauma was covered: the death of loved-ones, childhood deprivation, physical and sexual abuse, abortion, desertion, divorce, persecution, rape. It was an amazing education in how an individual can be influenced by an event of the distant past. Those who thought they had put 'it' behind them, found their emotions reawakened with overwhelming force. It taught me how powerful repressive mechanisms are, that they can relegate such suffering to the subconscious and keep it in check.

I sat near the back of the room, feeling inhibited and wondering what I was doing there. As time went on I developed a growing immunity and became increasingly fascinated. What would it be like to be on the mattress? A few times over the coming days I endeavoured to go forward, only to be overcome by anxiety. On the fourth day Phil served as my cue, making his way to the mattress and venting his rage at the church. My own feelings of anger surfaced and, as Phil finished, I rose and walked forward. I felt strangely dissociated, detached and isolated as I knelt on the mattress.

Like magic the truncheon appeared in my hand and a telephone directory opened in front of me. By the time I was finished, I had directed anger towards the medical establishment, my parents, my siblings and my wife, in fact towards just about everybody who had ever loved me. Eventually, exhausted by the effort, I slumped, kneeling and defeated. And yet, I didn't feel any different. It seemed to have been a worthless catharsis.

Elisabeth then asked everyone to take a break, indicating that I should stay. 'It is not anger that you need to deal with,' she said when we were alone. 'It is grief.' Elisabeth's presence was all around me and, as she spoke, it felt as if I was being cocooned in love and light. I was aware of her looking not at me but *into* me, and it seemed as if she was connecting her very soul with mine. 'Tell me of your losses. Who has died that you were close to?'

The most recent death had been my grandmother. In the distant past there was also my sister Julie, who died a 'cot death' when I was ten. We spoke of my relationship to both of them and of my feelings when they died. Elisabeth handed me a soft pillow to represent them, prompting me to talk to them, to tell them how I felt. I did so but it only seemed like 'going through the motions'. I wanted to cry but I couldn't. When it was apparent that I was stuck, Elisabeth's voice drifted in. 'There is a much deeper loss within you,' she said. 'Your greatest loss is not having unconditional love as a child. This is the deepest loss we all carry.'

The words were penetrating and affected me in an extra-ordinary way. I felt elevated, peaceful and blessed. A seed had been planted which germinated the following day, when one of the participants was grieving for a child killed in a boating accident. The little one's body had never been found, and the mother was re-living every vivid detail. As I sat in the middle of the room, I experienced a tearing emptiness inside me; the same hollow void that accompanied the knowledge that I would never see Julie again. Drawn into an abyss of guilt, shame and anguish, I rocked back and forth, hunched over, my face buried in my hands.

I regressed and was no longer a rational adult, blameless for his sister's death twenty years earlier. I became the child again, ten years-old, with my sister suffocating in the next room. It was my fault. Overwhelmed and irrational, I experienced a choking feeling as my heart broke. The catharsis that followed had an intensity that was greater than any single bereavement; it went beyond the loss of Julie. Julie was to be, in fact, the instrument that released me from repression and sorrow. I was about to realise that Julie had planted a seed of love and awareness which had remained dormant all these years. It was as if she herself was responsible for my spiritual awakening.

Once my heart had broken, it seemed to empty of sorrow and to open up. It was then, when I was completely vulnerable, that an incredible feeling of love and peacefulness began to flow into me, during which I seemed to detach from my physical body. There appeared to be light all around me, and a deep silence suffused with pure, unconditional love. Time stood still. It was as though a divine presence was filling every part of my being with unlimited love, until I felt merged and indivisible from it. It was an all-unifying experience during which I was somehow lifted beyond the material confines of our world. Later, when I 'returned' to the room, the feeling of contentment was awesome and beautiful. For the rest of the workshop, and the next few weeks, I remained in this elevated state with a feeling of radiant love for every human soul and every manifestation of nature.

It was as though a divine presence was filling every part of my being with unlimited love ...

The catharsis had brought enlightenment. Letting go of sorrow allowed me to glimpse the soul, its hidden nature and qualities. I now reflect on this as a 'spiritual window' through which I discovered my true identity, purpose and destiny; it showed me what I could become. As pure love was revealed to me after I 'let go', I knew that the love was always present, though hidden beneath layers of *acquired* pain.

In the same vein, when someone lets go and enters the state of acceptance before dying, I believe that they experience unconditional love and happiness.

FIVE

Acceptance

'My mother's peace was radiant and the room was filled with love.'

June was talking to me about her mother Margaret's death. When told that her ovarian cancer was incurable, Margaret was shocked and couldn't believe it. At first she thought that the doctors had made a mistake. Then, after realising it was true, she rejected the implication that she could die of it. As she deteriorated and this implication became real she got angry at the world: 'Why me?' she cried. June was often on the receiving end of this anger, which was followed by tears of guilt and remorse. Fortunately June was both loving and wise, and understood that her mother simply needed an outlet.

As Margaret became weaker, her anger gave way to depression and hopelessness. She began to grieve about the growing reality that she wouldn't be with her family for much longer. She had aimed to be around for her grandson's university graduation but now accepted that this would not be possible. Gradually, as she began to yield and give up the struggle, she started to accept what she had been fighting against. She would talk to June about what she wanted at her funeral and who was to receive various possessions. To everyone's amazement Margaret became happier and more contented as she faced her death. Instead of fearing it and struggling against its injustice, she let go and her suffering ended. She told June that 'dying is just like a walk in the park'.

June told me that she and her sisters were all present when Margaret was dying. 'It was beautiful,' she said. 'Mum had a presence about her and a contentment that made everybody feel uplifted and happy. I will never forget the power of the love that emanated from her. It was really special.'

Here, June was describing her mother's state of acceptance. I enquired further, 'At the end was she troubled by her looks and appearance, or about the disease and the fact that she was dying?'

June replied, 'No, mum was at peace with herself. Even though she was wasted, it was as if her body had ceased to exist. Only serenity remained and there was no fear in her at all.'

I next asked, 'Did your mother seem concerned or worried about any of you at that time.'

'No,' she replied. 'Mum knew we were there, but she seemed beyond any concern for how we were coping or feeling.'

'What about the problems of our world,' I asked. 'Was your mother affected by the deprivation and conflicts that are going on?' June smiled, then said, 'Mum always had a strong position on everything and used to get really agitated about such things. But, now you mention it, no she wasn't troubled at all. I guess she must have let go of everything.' June faltered for a moment, searching, then emotionally she repeated. '*She had let go of everything!*'

Finally I asked, 'After letting go, just before she died, did your mother seem burdened by any of the roles or responsibilities of her lifetime?'

'No,' she said. 'She had become free ... *completely free!*'

When someone is dying, it is a privilege when we witness this state of acceptance. In her final days, Margaret became free, her soul exposed before leaving the body. She was a gift to her family because she was revealing the truth of a spiritual identity that lies within. Through love and peace the soul was 'visible' and accessible to anyone who cared to be with her. June told me that the experience left her with a firm conviction about eternal life. It was, she said, as if her mother became a 'mirror', reflecting back the truth of the soul to those who visited her.

I regard this to be the character of true acceptance and would describe it as a state of liberation. June's mother is living proof that real dignity lies within the soul. Once liberated, despite being physically wasted and completely dependent, she gained grace and revealed her inner beauty. Her soul was liberated when it no longer had any interest in the body and its appearance; when it was no longer worried about roles and responsibilities; when it had let go of relationships; and when it was detached from the problems of an increasingly complex world.

Her presence filled the room with a radiance of love that reflected, I believe, a return to what she had once been — a peaceful soul.

Once free from concern about her body, the world and relationships, Margaret entered a state of being in which she was completely *soul-conscious*. Her presence filled the room with a radiance of love that reflected, I believe, a return to what she had once been — *a peaceful soul.*

In Margaret's experience we see how one's spiritual identity can surface in the face of death. The question is, do we have to wait until death to find serenity? And must we be forced into submission before we can love and let go? I now believe it possible to attain this liberation in life, and to rediscover our spiritual identity.

Let us now travel from one end of life to the other, where we will explore the quality of innocence and how it is 'lost' to the world we live in.

Innocence 'Lost'

On a national speaking tour around Australia, I asked audiences in every city to comment on what makes a newborn attractive. What is it about a baby, a puppy or a kitten that captures our hearts? The universal answer was innocence. Everybody also agreed that the quality of innocence embraces purity, openness, trust and vulnerability. When you think about it, we were all born like this. However, we knew nothing about the body or relationships and this inexperience rendered our innocence vulnerable. It is this ignorance, I believe, that leads us away from the soul's original nature of purity and peace.

One day, while sitting in a park, I was watching two children playing on the swings. Both were around two years-old. As they finished and headed off, their mothers suggested that they hold hands. The little girl happily linked hands with the little boy, whereupon he immediately threw her to the ground. She was inconsolable, not from being physically hurt but from the shock. It had been totally unexpected. The boy was reprimanded, as the girl was comforted. Then, when they were ready to leave, the boy's mother told him to hold her hand again, properly. 'Innocently' he held out his hand to her.

No way! She stepped back, withdrew her hands and put them behind her back. She had learnt fear. Having experienced betrayal she was unwilling to trust and found it necessary to protect herself. She was not as innocent as she had been before the incident. Now more experienced, she would no longer be so unconditional and open with her trust. A small impression of doubt and uncertainty about relationships had been imprinted on her mind, and a small layer of defensiveness was now in her character. Although she had become less vulnerable, a tiny part of her inner beauty had been blemished.

Consider for a moment the vast challenges we face in our lives. Although we have many experiences of joy and happiness, how many undermining encounters have we had? All of us go through different forms of physical, mental or emotional pain at some time or another. Extrapolating from the little girl, it doesn't take long to realise that our original personality is modified by experience. As we layer ourselves with defences and withdraw our trust and openness, innocence is lost.

We are also conditioned to think of ourselves as physical beings, adopting an identity that reflects name and bodily form. To begin with, this identity is relatively simple but, in time, it becomes more complex. Through it we learn to separate and discriminate on the basis of gender, familiar relationships, skin colour and culture. We develop a sense of individuality and, with it, desires to have or to possess for the self. As ego develops in this way, so the pursuit of self-gratification makes us increasingly dependent and creates expanding needs. We also become more fearful due to the potential for loss or deprivation when our desires go unfulfilled.

A child can be happy for no reason. In time, however, happiness becomes dependent on fulfilling desires. We forget the love which is intrinsic to the soul and begin to seek it on the outside. Eventually our ability to experience peace, happiness and love is surrendered to the stability of external circumstances and relationships.

At birth our state of being is what can be referred to as

soul-consciousness; it is innocent yet ignorant of the world. In time, the soul is deceived as it develops what can be termed *body-consciousness* and ego. When this happens we become dependent on health, wealth, status and relationships to feel loved, valued and secure. As these are subject to change and fluctuation, so too are our peace and happiness, and our contentment comes under constant threat.

To ward off insecurity we develop negative attributes such as greed, possessiveness and anger, which either sustain us or make us feel more in control of our world. However, when they fail us and we lose control of our circumstances, we can become anxious, stressed, desperate or depressed.

All this represents body-consciousness, which is like a veil shrouding the true and original identity of a soul. Yet the peace, love and purity, and the openness, trust and innocence of our original nature (our soul-consciousness) has not been lost. It is the hidden truth that lies within — a truth we see revealed once again, when a soul is returned to love in the state of acceptance.

It is, I believe, this 'veil' of body-consciousness that Kübler-Ross identified as unfinished business. And it is behind this veil that purity hides. I am fortunate that she had this insight and showed health professionals a way to discover their truth. My experience of soul-consciousness followed a catharsis, proving to me that our innocence is preserved and can re-emerge. When this happens in life it is experienced as enlightenment which, paradoxically, means only to rediscover who we were.

To grow spiritually we need to let go of our conditioning and break down our body-consciousness. While we can

My experience of soul-consciousness followed a catharsis, proving to me that our innocence is preserved and can re-emerge.

learn from acceptance there is surely a better way than dying to renew our innocence. I would suggest adopting a spiritual life that allows us to develop self-awareness whilst relating to a higher power.

It would also be helpful to have some more objective evidence for a spiritual dimension, including an afterlife.

SEVEN

Afterlife

J often ask patients if they have any philosophy or beliefs about what happens after we die. Not infrequently they smile and say, 'Nobody has ever come back to tell us, have they?' I think they're mistaken. In fact I believe that contact is frequently made by souls after they have left the body. There is a huge body of literature about metaphysical and paranormal phenomena, ranging from out-of-body experiences to apparitions and 'miracles'. Nevertheless, as this is all anecdotal and doesn't prove the existence of the soul, most people remain cynical. Minds only open after significant and validating spiritual experiences.

Studies have confirmed the frequent occurrence of paranormal experiences across many cultures. Random sampling of the general population in countries that included USA, Great Britain, Germany, Italy and Iceland concluded that more than a quarter of subjects had had a paranormal experience.

One striking anecdotal report appeared in the *Lancet* medical journal (J. M. Small, 'Sixth Sense', *Lancet*, vol. 337, 1991, p. 1550). A neurosurgeon, who describes himself as pragmatic, recounts the following experience:

> When I opened the kitchen door all appeared normal but then there seemed to be a curious descending dark shimmer in the far part of the kitchen, immediately gone but I knew it was death and female … As I reached the bedroom, the doorbell rang and I was not surprised to see the village policeman who said he would be grateful for my help.

The doctor then explains how the policeman had been on his way to tell his neighbour that her sister was seriously ill. Just as the policeman arrived he received a radio message that the woman had died. Knowing that the doctor lived next door he called to seek help in dealing with this sensitive matter. The doctor concluded: 'There was a message in my mind. How it reached there is not defined. Although first confused with fear, it was so very clear.'

A survey conducted by Dr Michael Barbato, in Sydney, documents paranormal experiences in relatives after their next of kin had died. It shows that paranormal phenomena, such as a vision of the person who died, occurred in at least eighteen per cent of cases. A patient's daughter related one such instance to me. Although her father was jaundiced and wasted, she told me how wonderful it was to be present at his death. She said that she 'saw' his soul leaving the body. It was only momentary but there was an instant where she witnessed his passage. Her mother, on the other hand, was haunted by the memory of his physical appearance, and her grief was intense for the first two months. Then one night he appeared to her, standing at the foot of her bed, smiling and in full health. Although he didn't try to communicate, she felt warm, peaceful and happy. By the time he disappeared, he had deleted the image of his dying body from her mind and left her knowing that she would see him again one day. The intensity of her grief diminished overnight.

It is also common for someone close to death to have visions of relatives who have already died. Sometimes, when I'm sitting by a patient's bed, I notice the person looking at or talking to someone who 'isn't there'. One lady who had been unconscious, suddenly sat up looking at an empty chair in the corner and said, 'Oh, it's you,' then lapsed back into a coma. I believe that spirits are sometimes attracted to visit and comfort the dying during the terminal phase. A relatively frequent occurrence is the apparition of a child.

On one such occasion a forty year-old patient and her husband had been independently seeing a little girl. It began in the last three to four months of Joy's life with multiple myeloma, a cancer of the bone marrow. 'She used to come and look in through the window,' Joy told me. 'She was very pretty, about six years of age and always had a smiling face. When I went to the window and looked out there was no one there. One day I noticed David staring at her too and I said: 'You can see her can't you?' It turned out that David had been seeing her the whole time but neither of them had told the other. They hadn't wanted to alarm each other. It became a very comforting experience for them and it proved to both of them that there was an after-life. How can two people independently have the same hallucination? Clearly the child was real and spiritual.

For me, existence of the afterlife was confirmed by one significant experience. Trudy came to see me with her husband, Jim, who was in his mid-forties with advanced bowel cancer. He was wasted and terminally ill. Troubled by recurrent bowel obstructions and painful pelvic disease, Jim was depressed by his condition, while Trudy was a dedicated carer whose love, commitment and tolerance knew no boundaries. She was also a registered nurse working in the operating theatres of a local district hospital.

Jim was dealing with his situation in a somewhat intellectual manner. He carefully guarded his feelings and avoided vulnerability. He did, however, fully acknowledge his disease and the implications of it being incurable. With this understanding and his strong intellect, Jim was a fighter who would never give in. Wanting to live for as long as possible there was no way he was going to lie down and die.

Jim, Trudy and I were sitting in an outpatient consultation room. We had spent some time going over recent problems and I had just outlined a new management plan to address these. At that point I asked Jim how he had been coping mentally, expecting him to say, 'fine, no problems'. To my surprise he opened up for the first time, saying that he was upset about his adolescent children. Knowing that he wouldn't be around in the future, Jim was driving their maturation. He was trying to fulfil in months a role that he might have played over the next ten years. Being in their early teens, however, the children were at a stage of develop-ment where they could accept parental support and guid-ance but not direction. Conflict arose as they refused to allow Jim to direct their lives and future career options. He became very depressed about it.

While I was listening to Jim's story, I began to experience a very deep and empathic bond to him. In fact I was so engaged by him that the world around seemed silent and distant. As I took my turn to speak, Trudy seemed remote and only on the fringe of my awareness. I pointed out the problems I saw in Jim's endeavours. Though understand-able, it was placing his children under too much pressure, and it would be better to ease back a little. I went on to say how I felt he would fulfil their needs in the future.

'Jim, when someone dies while we are still young he or she leaves behind a "seed", which germinates in its own time. I once had a sister who died when I was ten years-old. She left in me a potential that I realised twenty years later …' I went on to relate some of the Kübler-Ross experience covered in Chapter 4, then concluded: 'Julie died but the seed she left behind eventually led to my enlightenment. It was a gift far greater than she could have managed if she had lived. She became, in effect, my guide and teacher in later life. Likewise, Jim, give your children love and a relationship free from expectations. In this way, you will accompany them through their lives and give them more than your physical guidance ever could.'

While I was speaking there was a sensation of love and peace, connecting and surrounding us. I had only a distant sense of my own body and felt an exquisite lightness of spirit. It seemed like a silent, powerful, healing presence was with us. Such was the intensity of my connection to Jim that Trudy had become virtually 'non-existent'.

After the consultation I was given a message from Trudy asking me to contact her. She had to speak to me about something that happened while we were together. Trudy was nervous when I called and sounded me out to see if she could say what she needed to. I prompted her but nothing could have prepared me for what she would say; or the dilemma it would create.

'When you started sharing your experiences with Jim, a little girl came into the room. She was quite beautiful and light; and about seven years-old. She danced around you the whole time and it seems that you have a special connection with her. She was happy to be close to you and really joyful that I could see her. She told me that she wants you to tell her parents that she is happy and dancing again. Who could she be?' I was a bit too surprised to entertain that question immediately, so I asked one of my own. 'Well what does she look like and where is she now?' Trudy described her, giving special attention to a unique curl in her hair, which dipped over her forehead. I couldn't think of anyone matching the description. As for where she was now, 'Right here with me,' said Trudy. 'She stayed with me and won't leave until I have done what she wants.' Trudy seemed matter-of-fact so I asked, 'Has this sort of thing happened before and can't you ask her who she is?'

She explained, 'Yes, it happens from time to time. When a spirit comes, it stays with me until I satisfy its wishes or refuse to comply. I comply unless it is malevolent, in which case I turn my back to make it go away. They don't actually speak in words but my understanding couldn't be any clearer if they did. I can't speak to them so it's not possible for me to ask questions. It always ends up being a bit of a puzzle like this, I'm afraid.'

'Why didn't you tell me earlier?' I asked.

'I didn't know how you'd react. You don't just come out and say things like this to a doctor. So I thought it safer to tell your secretary first. In fact she told me there was a girl of around this age under your care a year ago.' I cast my mind back and remembered the child in question. 'Yes, little Tegan Sowry. But she bore no resemblance to the description you just gave me.'

'It's her,' Trudy exclaimed.

'How can you say that?' I asked. Trudy was laughing on the other end of the phone. 'Because,' she replied, 'when you said her name, she jumped up and down, clapping her hands. She's so happy now.' I considered this and then asked, 'So what am I supposed to do now?'

'Ring her mother,' Trudy replied.

'You're kidding,' I protested. 'I can't do that. I've no idea what's happened there since Tegan died. And I don't even know for sure it's her.'

'Just ring her and see,' said Trudy, clearly amused by my confusion.

After hanging up I thought about Tegan. I only visited her once, towards the end of her illness. After that I stayed in touch with her mother and the family doctor by phone. Tegan had a degenerative, neurological condition that affected her from the age of four. She gradually lost mobility and the capacity to communicate. When I saw her she was seven years-old and couldn't walk, talk or do anything for herself. She was chair-bound and completely dependent on her mother. There was nothing I could think of that resembled Trudy's description.

I also had another dilemma. How would her mother react to me telling her this story? I had no idea what problems it might cause the family. They might not believe it and I had no way of knowing whether it would cause further distress. On the other hand I had had a good rapport with Beth, Tegan's mother, and I remembered that she had a strong spiritual side to her. On these two accounts, I felt that it would do no harm to at least contact her.

I phoned her to arrange a meeting. She was happy to hear from me but wary, and couldn't understand why I wanted to meet her. Rather awkwardly, I decided to discuss it with her over the phone. I said that Tegan had made contact with me, through a nurse who was psychic. I went on to describe what had happened. Beth interrupted me briefly, 'Tegan loved to dance before she got too sick,' she said. As I was giving her the description, Beth exclaimed. 'I always used to do her hair that way, with a little curl over her forehead! It made her look so sweet.'

By this stage I started to get goosebumps. At the point where the little girl jumped up and down clapping, Beth just said, 'Oh, my dear God. That's exactly what she used to do when she was happy or excited. It's definitely her. I've just got goosebumps all over.'

'Me too,' I said, relieved now that her identity was clear. 'Tegan asked me to give you a message. She wants you to know that she is happy and dancing again. You don't have to feel sad any more.'

Beth wanted to speak to Trudy, so I gave her the contact number. They spoke together and were able to confirm Tegan's identity with an old photograph. Tegan herself took leave of Trudy when I was speaking to her mother. She has never tried to make contact again.

As for Jim, he defied all expectations and lived for another year. By letting go of his need to be 'a good father' he actually succeeded in this endeavour. Trudy and I still have contact with one another, in the bond that was tied by Tegan.

Tegan demonstrates a potential beyond all physical

limitations. She appeared to Trudy in a non-physical form of light. Within this her psyche was intact and her individuality maintained. She was also still attached to her family and had the desire to relieve her mother's grief.

There are two things which validated Tegan's apparition, and demonstrated that death is but a separation of 'the self' and the body. Neither Trudy nor I could identify the child who presented features and mannerisms that were only known to her mother. When I had visited Tegan she had been paralysed and bed-bound. Even if I had seen an old photograph there was no way I could have known her mannerism of happiness. There is no doubt that Tegan was real.

She is also evidence that we are more than a physical body. She appeared in an ethereal form of light with the identity of her recent life. Not only do we exist after death but we also maintain our identity. As she left the physical body in her ethereal form, it stands to reason that these are superimposed during 'life' and separate at 'death'. It is quite possible that the 'light' people experience in 'out-of-body' and near-death experiences is their own ethereal form. It is also quite possible that we can learn to experience our light form through meditation and other spiritual practices.

Not only do we exist after death but we also maintain our identity.

I am now certain that there is life after death, and that there is purpose, reason or meaning behind everything I witness or experience. In fact I no longer believe in death as a reality. Mortality is a reflection of limited perception. If we open our minds and listen with our souls then we will realise that they really do come back to tell us, don't they?

EIGHT

Enlightenment

Spirituality is relatively unimportant to most people's lives. The experience of enlightenment can change this, as there is no turning away from the spiritual insight it brings. It is best considered a gift, substantiating an existence that is not confined to the physical plane.

The two main features of enlightenment are *experience* and *recognition* — the experience of love, peace and purity, and the recognition that these are qualities of the soul or of a higher power.

A few years ago I saw Joe, a truck driver who was married and in his mid-fifties. A local doctor requested a home visit, as Joe was in too much pain to come to the hospital. He had a modest homestead set in natural rainforest, several kilometres from any main roads. I arrived at the homestead on a cool spring morning. Closing the car door, I was enveloped by complete silence as I stood in the tidy well-kept garden.

The serenity and beauty of the garden was a striking contrast to the atmosphere within the household. When his wife Anne opened the door, her sunken face, furrowed brow and the dark shadows around her eyes revealed her exhaustion. She was at the end of her tether.

Lying on the lounge, Joe was calm enough until he moved to greet me. The effort brought on a severe spasm of pain in his buttocks and legs. He exhaled sharply and carefully settled himself back into a more comfortable position. I administered a morphine injection for pain control, then explained my role and why I had been asked to see him. Joe relaxed, indicating that the morphine was taking effect.

He had had a successful operation for bladder cancer three years earlier, but relapsed two years later with secondary cancer in the spine. Radiotherapy provided relief at first but the cancer spread progressively to involve more of the bones in his lower back and pelvis. In the last two months he had experienced increasingly severe chronic pain, only partially relieved by further radiotherapy. Despite oral morphine, the pain became almost incapacitating when he moved. Worse still, he became breathless — an X-ray revealed secondary cancers in his lungs. Joe would not live very much longer.

After reviewing his medications, I was confident I could improve the situation. I thought he would be able to have much greater freedom of movement, with the prospect of a better quality of life. Joe was encouraged, relieved by the idea that he would not have to keep on suffering to the end. I asked him how he viewed his current circumstances.

He immediately volunteered that he couldn't see himself living much longer. Joe was keen to discuss the subject of dying, which everyone, to his frustration, had been avoiding. I asked him how he felt about dying. He said he was not afraid, especially now that he understood the pain could be controlled. I then asked if he had any particular beliefs or philosophy that had made the idea more comfortable to him.

As he hesitated and I waited, the room seemed to become still and peaceful around us. Joe told me there had been an experience which he had never shared with anyone. He had thought that no one would believe him, and had worried about appearing foolish. With genuine interest I prompted him. When he was thirty-two, Joe had had an operation to repair a simple hernia in his left groin. In the post-operative recovery room he had had a cardiac arrest and 'died'. He felt himself float out of his body towards to the ceiling. There followed an extraordinary sensation of serenity, as he was surrounded in golden-white light. He felt blissful, free and liberated, yet alert and fully aware without any bodily sensations.

Down below he observed resuscitation attempts on his physical body, while up above he could see a swirling light that appeared to be beckoning. For just a moment there seemed a choice, which ended abruptly as he was shocked back into the physical, searing pain in his chest and struggling to breathe. Yet strangely he felt detached, with no fear of death despite the unpleasant sensations and effects of resuscitation. He had never feared death from that day on.

He felt blissful, free and liberated, yet alert and fully aware without any bodily sensations.

For Joe this experience established, beyond doubt, the existence of a spiritual dimension. His nature changed considerably as a consequence. Joe became less of a perfectionist, more at ease and more tolerant. He said that others found him to be more dependable and stable in comparison with his pre-operative personality. Up to the day of my visit, he had kept this all to himself, fearing derision, rejection or mockery. Now, in the face of death, sharing the experience left him joyful, as he again tasted the reality of his soul. Joe had described both the experience and the recognition that characterise enlightenment. He was aware that he was eternal and that the change in him was clearly visible to others. Afraid of rejection however, he didn't explore the experience or its implications any further.

This keeps the potential within enlightenment dormant, whereas deeper recognition of its spiritual implications and a willingness to change oneself leads to the path of *realisation*. This path is also accessible to anyone who has spiritual insight and the desire to reach his or her full potential.

NINE

The Path of Realisation

The word recognition means 'to know again' or 'to identify as known before'. It is very easy to apply this to something physical, such as a possession or an old friend. What is more challenging, yet just as relevant, is to apply recognition to one's 'inner self'. In the preceding chapters I have encouraged the reader to think of spiritual identity as something that is modified by life experience. I truly believe that we 'forget' who we are in the course of our lives.

When there is enlightenment, one is really recognising ('knowing again', or 'identifying as known before') the true and original nature of the soul. Recognition implies that this is nothing new and that spiritual growth is a paradoxical process in which we return to our original nature. The word realisation means 'to make real' or 'to bring into fact'. As we realise our spiritual identity, it is 'made real' and becomes apparent. When thought of in these terms we begin to see an enticing possibility — that truth resides within us and that its realisation reveals our spiritual identity.

The journey or path of realisation is one of inner healing and renewal, which enables us to be open and loving, without vulnerability or dependency. It could be viewed as a journey in which we return to a pure form and expression of love that is both unconditional and spiritual. The path of realisation, whether through faith or enlightenment, requires both spiritual awareness and personal endeavour. We need to make an effort to hold onto peace and spiritual values, whilst living in a world that constantly challenges these.

I believe this state of realisation to be more important than the belief systems or religions that we follow. Values inherent to love are the essence and common aim of all religions. Whether discovered through a particular spiritual path or on the basis of personal experience, such values express our spirituality. I also believe that everyone has a spiritual path, which remains latent until something awakens us to it. Hidden within each person is the original nature of the soul waiting to be experienced, recognised and realised.

Hidden within each person is the original nature of the soul waiting to be experienced, recognised and realised.

Emotional pain, fear and repression separate us from experiencing this inherent beauty. If we can reverse the conditioning of our lives, then we can realise the truth that resides within us. The path of realisation is a journey within, to engage the intrinsic divinity of the soul.

I shall now be looking at the efforts required to transform weaknesses that separate us from experiencing love, unity and peace. These will be seen as conditioned and habitual personality traits that were not part of our original nature. As such traits are acquired through the mistaken identity of body-consciousness, they can be transformed through spiritual knowledge and awareness.

TEN

Meditation

Until experiencing spiritual love at the Kübler-Ross workshop, I was a confirmed atheist. Afterwards, by contrast, I believed that God had touched my life, revealing a quality of love that I should sustain and share with others. To hold and maintain this relationship with love, however, was to prove challenging.

To begin with, I changed two things in my life. The first was my career as a cancer specialist. Up to the workshop, I had given little consideration to the suffering aspect of cancer. Afterwards I had a genuine wish to relieve my patient's physical and emotional pain. With compassion awoken, serving others gave me pleasure and I was drawn to work with the dying. This brought me a sense of being more holistic and complete as a physician. The other change I made involved taking up meditation, so as to care for myself whilst caring for others. I found the balance of meditation and service to be a most effective way of nurturing love.

I taught myself to meditate by reading about it and practising daily. My aim was to feel connected in love to God, as this is what I believed I had experienced at the workshop. I used to sit on an escarpment close to my home overlooking a forest canopy and the ocean. On reflection, I am amused when I recall my intensity and desire for an experience of God. I would sit for an hour a day, eyes closed, trying to reach God. Generally I became very peaceful and contented, but I never had the rush of love that I experienced with Kübler-Ross.

One day it occurred to me that maybe God was trying to reach me, and all I had to do was allow Him/Her to do so. On that occasion I just opened my heart and, with a feeling of surrender, was immediately filled with love. This sense of 'allowing God' is subtly different because it is based 'on God's terms' rather than mine. I began to see that my own ego had been separating me from love and that this was a block I needed to address.

To guide my mind in a more spiritual direction, I started to read from uplifting texts for around twenty minutes during meditation. These put me in touch with my eternal identity, made me feel connected with God's love, and gave me a sense of serving humanity. During the day I would reflect on the morning reading, which kept the meditation experience alive through my working hours. I began thus to integrate spiritual values into daily living, which accords with the Eastern term for religion (dharma) that means 'way of life'.

About eight years after the workshop with Kübler-Ross, a doctor working under my supervision introduced me to some new concepts. She believed the soul could become impure and that it thinks, speaks and acts through the instrument or vehicle of the body. The original purity and peace of the soul is suppressed as its behaviour is conditioned by body-consciousness. She said that the soul becomes flawed and that meditation reverses this conditioning towards purity again. Meditation, she told me, is about channelling thoughts in the 'right' direction and about mastering our minds and senses. Thoughts are our creation and they determine how

Meditation, she told me, is about channelling thoughts in the 'right' direction and about mastering our minds and senses.

we feel. If they were not so influenced by the external world, and were less drawn towards various forms of sense-gratification, then we would feel peaceful and loving.

Although I resisted these ideas, they gradually made sense. I had believed the soul to be ever-pure and beyond worldly influence, just waiting for me to find it. Now I began to think: 'Who am "I" and who is the soul?' I remember walking into a patient's room just after he had died. There was a distinct sense of the presence of that departed spirit as I examined the body. I could feel his personality in the room, yet the body was lifeless. The body had no attitudes, memories or identity without the soul; nor could it communicate. The soul had left with its individuality and personality intact. I now believed what my friend had told me and my question was answered: 'I am a soul and I act through my body.'

The challenging thing about holding and maintaining a relationship with love is that we constantly separate ourselves from it. Whenever we react to criticism, become angry or spread unkind gossip we separate ourselves from love. Whenever we feel jealous or depressed we separate ourselves from love. Whenever we are forceful or afraid, we separate ourselves from love. Meditation, as a way of life, changes the way we react and how we are influenced. On the basis of spiritual awareness and attitudes, it gives us the power to focus our minds in the positive direction of peace and happiness. If we stop the thoughts that create stress and negativity, then we are likely to have a beneficial influence on others without trying.

Meditation makes the mind receptive to love, not simply as an emotion but as a power to do good. In the coming chapters we will look at forms of effort-making that enable the soul to remain peaceful and connected with love. In my first encounter with unconditional love, love was my whole experience. For three weeks after the cathartic workshop,

I was love. It was a state of being. In the last six years I have practised a form of meditation that encourages one to transform negative characteristics, whilst adopting spiritual values. In this spiritual endeavour, the first step is to understand the mind and its potential. The second is to heal oneself. And the third is to become love.

ELEVEN

Spiritual Effort: Appreciation

When I first met Margo she was fifty-three and had been diagnosed with breast cancer for four years. Although initially slow-growing, the disease had become more aggressive over the last year. Despite several courses of chemotherapy it had spread to her liver and lungs. We discussed her illness, life and family; her aspirations and disappointments.

She had divorced ten years earlier, retaining custody of her only daughter Genaro. They were inseparable. Her greatest regret was leaving Genaro and not seeing her grandchildren grow up. She felt all right about dying but was distressed for her family. 'I can't bear to see them so upset about me,' she once confided.

Margo had spent a year of her adolescence living amongst indigenous Native North Americans. As a result, she became something of a spiritual eccentric in her adult life. With respect for the land and all its creatures, she believed her spirit would return to the earth, living on in the forest, in the wind and in the sea. She would visit her family and meet with elders of the spirit world. As her first love was nature, she wished to be cremated on an open woodpile in the forest.

When Margo was dying she needed assistance to walk, shower and toilet. I had taken to visiting her at home rather than seeing her in outpatients. She lived in a house under a rocky escarpment, in dense bushland with elevated sea-views. Genaro had moved in to look after her. When I called one November morning, Genaro's smiling face greeted me. She looked calm. I asked her how her mum was.

'Go see for yourself,' she replied. 'Out in the garden. I'll leave you two alone.' The garden typified Margo's character. Tidy shrubs and rockeries decorated the upper tier. The lower tier was wild with native gums adjoining a narrow stream, where a lizard was sunning itself on a rock, as bird-life quietly fluttered here and there. With the escarpment rising above, it seemed the perfect setting for being at one with nature.

Margo was seated in the shade on the upper tier. Facing the stream and the escarpment, she didn't see me as I walked from the patio. Despite her disease and dependency, Margo still looked reasonably well. As I approached her, she seemed completely absorbed in the beauty of her garden. There was something about her facial expression that I couldn't quite grasp; a stillness or an aura of gentleness. Noticing me, she smiled and in a moment of eye contact I suddenly realised what I saw in her. It was more than peace, more than happiness. *It was profound contentment.* She appeared 'at one' with the universe, and things were clearly different for her now compared with the troubled Margo of two weeks ago.

Returning the smile, I greeted her and sat down. 'Margo, you seem completely absorbed in the beauty of your garden.' Still smiling through soft grey eyes, she replied, 'No, it is the beauty of my self that I am absorbed in.' She sighed happily and continued.

'In all these years that I have loved nature, I never realised it was my "self" that I was appreciating. I would go to the forest to feel peaceful, the sea to find beauty or the mountains to experience wonder. Every time I went somewhere like this I would become happy and uplifted.

'Only now have I understood why. I have realised that what I experienced in relation to nature was within myself. When I went to these places all the conflicts and problems of my life disappeared temporarily. When I looked in awe at a mountain the sight was free from sentiment, yet I experienced wonder.'

I must have been looking puzzled.

'Don't you see,' she said. 'The wonder was not in the mountain, it was in me! When we go to these places we become free from all the superficial things of life. This freedom makes our spirit happy and we experience love, peace and simplicity. If we could only learn to listen to our spirit then we could remain absorbed in its beauty.' She paused, slightly breathless from her lung disease.

'In all these years that I have loved nature, I never realised it was my "self" that I was appreciating.'

'For all my life I have been dependent on nature to be happy. At least up until now. It is as if I was searching on the outside for what made me feel good on the inside. You discover your soul when you find and appreciate your inner beauty. We must take peace from the forest and own it, because in truth it really belongs to us. Nature's gift is what it awakens in us.'

Margo seemed oblivious to a butterfly that had landed on the back of her hand. Lazily it opened and closed iridescent blue wings as she continued.

'I am going to die soon,' she smiled, then qualified, 'Well, I am going across the threshold that some people call death. I would like to have lived a little longer to give this message to the world: to appreciate that everything we really need is already within us. At least I have discovered it for myself. Perhaps you could spread it around for me.'

'I'll write a book about it,' I joked. We laughed. 'You don't really need anything from me, do you?' I asked.

'No,' she replied. 'Just the book!'

As I walked away I glanced back. The look of deep content-ment had returned. She was beautiful and at peace with herself. The butterfly left her hand, hovered for a few moments then flew away. Margo died two hours later.

I was deeply affected by Margo's contentment and its lesson: *appreciate your intrinsic beauty and you will become deeply contented.* We are coloured by the circumstances of our lives. Beautiful scenery in the absence of pressure draws peace, happiness and well-being to the surface. Difficult relationships, conflict and responsibilities make us feel trapped, tense or unhappy. It is as if, when a scene changes, our contentment can either surface or become merged within us. Imagine having the power to maintain it under any circumstances. Instead of being 'coloured', our content-ment would have a positive influence on our world and relationships. As Margo said, we must take peace from the forest and own it, because in truth it really belongs to us.

When we have the awareness that real identity is soul, then this is expressed through spirituality in our attitudes, actions and relationships. Spirituality really means inner beauty revealed in a 'visible' expression of virtues. If you relate *constantly* with peace, understanding, wisdom and mercy, then you will be influential on the basis of spirituality. Others will trust in your love and acceptance of them. It is such a personality that the effort of appreciation leads to.

Appreciation involves looking for strengths beyond the mistakes and weaknesses we witness. All too often we look for, and speak of, the negative characteristics of others. We take 'on board' their negativity, spread it around with gossip and lose our peace of mind in doing so. We might feel justified but what good has been done? Likewise, as our own weaknesses or mistakes hurt us, we tend to think more of these than of our qualities, strengths and virtues. The effort of appreciation is a decision to look only at virtues within the self and others. It is a decision to ignore the inner critic that says, 'I'm no good,' or 'They're no good'.

Behind the facades of ego or arrogance, every human soul is beautiful. Body-conscious conditioning conceals spiritual love and innocence, enabling negativity to surface. Whatever the words or actions, beauty resides within. Hidden away. However hard it is to believe at times, there are no exceptions. A key aspect to appreciating the beauty of your soul is to understand and accept this. As you discover this beauty within yourself, you will find it in others. If you refuse to see it in others, you will be unable to find it in yourself.

By seeking virtues in others, you learn more of the qualities they define and you are able to imbibe them for yourself. Say, for instance, that your boss is a successful businessman but his greed has affected his employees. He is also a very determined character who, by satisfying himself, has been using his determination in a negative and destructive way. To react to his greed by criticising his attitude and integrity, brings you into angry or jealous feelings. In 'choosing' this response you 'decide' to become 'peaceless', without influencing his behaviour. Furthermore you are attacking a human soul who is lost and blind; lost behind the veils of body-consciousness and blinded by material desires. His greed has affected you and you have allowed your peace of mind to dissolve.

If, instead, you remain unaffected by his greed but absorb the quality of determination, then three things change in the relationship. First, you maintain your peace of mind; second, you add to your beauty by imbibing the virtue of determination; and third, you have *given* him regard by appreciating his quality.

Although the businessman has distorted the value of determination through greed, it is actually a surviving, still-visible virtue. It can still be seen in his personality and, in all likelihood, it is this *virtue* that has enabled him to succeed. We can think of it as one of the specialities of his soul.

With purer soul-conscious motives, determination is a virtue of divine purpose. Determination to see value in everything. Determination never to give sorrow to anyone. Determination to maintain a positive attitude. Determination to grow. If you take the quality and disengage it from the greed, then you learn about it, reawaken it in yourself and become more virtuous.

The pure state of soul-consciousness is complete with all divine virtues, whereas in body-consciousness, virtues become hidden or distorted. Fortunately the distortion is not in the virtue itself but is in the motive with which it is used. The effort of appreciation is a spiritual endeavour of finding and expressing our virtues in a beneficial way.

... gentleness, respect and humility emerge with the courage and confidence to be ourselves.

Like anything else, practice makes perfect. If I wanted to be good on the piano I would need to take lessons and practise regularly. At first it would require concentration and would feel awkward. In time, however, playing would become natural with little need to think or concentrate. The same is true of virtues; they can be practised until they become a natural expression of ourselves.

As we reconnect with these original qualities, gentleness, respect and humility emerge with the courage and confidence to be ourselves. From this deep sense of self-respect we can give regard to others unconditionally, and become profoundly contented. As I experienced in Margo's company, such contentment is extremely attractive and influential. It is like a spiritual 'fragrance' that naturally serves others while you are simply being yourself.

In accepting only virtues from the outside world we are learning to see differently. Both effort and attention are necessary to sustain this divine vision and to maintain the contentment it offers. In the next chapter we will look at the application of meditation to this end.

TWELVE

Meditation Exercise: Imbibing and Developing Virtues

I n this exercise I will first outline a way of entering meditation, then focus on the aspect of virtues. I have listed thirty-six virtues below, taken from my study of Raja Yoga meditation. These might prove useful as you concentrate on those you either feel familiar with or need to acquire.

Your Divine Virtues

Cheerfulness	Introspection	Maturity
Sweetness	Tolerance	Humility
Honesty	Mercy	Lightness
Fearlessness	Contentment	Patience
Wisdom	Self-Confidence	Purity
Benevolence	Generosity	Truthfulness
Tirelessness	Obedience	Royalty (of self)
Accuracy	Surrender	Carefree
Courage	Discipline	Cleanliness
Stability	Gentleness	Determination
Detachment	Simplicity	Cooperation
Respect	Serenity	Flexibility

As we practise particular virtues we become more familiar with them and learn how to use them. Ultimately they give power to our minds, with the capacity to maintain equanimity whilst having constant good wishes for others.

To begin with, sit quietly and comfortably somewhere. If you already have a meditation technique, then enter meditation in the usual way. If not, then try the following ideas to relax the body and become peaceful. It is preferable to meditate with the eyes open, as what we learn is to be applied to everyday living.

Sit comfortably and with the body alert and symmetrical. Let your mind first go over the body, relaxing each part, from the feet up. It can be helpful to tense and relax each part, and to experience the difference between tension and relaxation. As you proceed you will find yourself entering a progressively deeper state of deep relaxation.

Beginning with the feet, followed by the calves; first tense then relax the muscles, and feel the difference that relaxation brings. Next, the thighs: relax the muscles, letting the tension go; then the buttocks: tense the muscles and relax, letting the tension go. Allow the feeling of relaxation to spread through you.

Repeat this exercise on the stomach, the chest, the shoulders, the upper arms, the forearms and the hands. After tensing and relaxing the hands, spend a few moments just observing where they are resting, and feel deep relaxation spreading through you. A feeling of letting all tension go, now the neck. Then the jaw: grit the teeth together tightly, then let the mouth hang slightly open. Next, the eyes. I always found this an amazingly relaxing sensation by this stage. Screw up the eyes tightly, hold the tension, then let it go. And finally the forehead: frowning tensely and letting go.

Once the body is relaxed, sit for a few minutes absorbing yourself into the experience of relaxation. Whilst in this state have the thought, 'I am a peaceful soul,' and simply sit, observing how relaxed the body feels.

Next go into experiencing a virtue or quality you would like to develop. Take for instance the virtue of tolerance. The stronger you are in this, the less likely you are to resort to anger. First think about the quality, then go into its experience. There are several ways of doing this. If you are tolerant by nature then it is a quite accessible virtue and you can enter its experience directly. If it is less familiar, you can find it by visualising someone you know with a tolerant nature, and then enter the feeling of tolerance in that person's character. This draws your latent tolerance to the surface, and very soon you begin to experience the state of tolerance itself.

Once you are experiencing the quality, next consider its value. Again there are several ways of doing this. You can imagine yourself in a situation where it is needed and visualise yourself using the quality effectively. Alternatively, remember a situation where you became angry. Bring that situation to mind, then imagine using tolerance and visualise a better outcome. In this you are not trying to change what happened but are converting a negative experience into one of learning.

In this way, through meditation, you practise and experience virtues, as well as learn how to use them. By becoming familiar with the qualities you need for different situations, they become much easier to access when challenged. In choosing to remain virtuous throughout the day, you will also find that you are much more in control of yourself.

For this exercise, first consider, and write down, the virtues or qualities which are your strongest. You might like to refer to the list I have given or use your own words. The ones that feel familiar to you are your strongest virtues. Of the others, write down three or four you would particularly like to work on.

Apply the meditation exercise to one virtue at a time, beginning with the more familiar ones. It is useful to look up the dictionary definition, as this will give you a better feel for the nature and quality of each one. Spend fifteen or twenty minutes in the morning with the exercise. During the day, be aware of every time you use the virtue you are working on. In the evening spend another fifteen to twenty minutes of meditation or reflection to review the day. Go again into the experience of the virtue and feel what it was like to use it. Also review situations where it would have been useful (or where you should have used it), and visualise yourself applying it. It is good to keep a diary as a way of monitoring progress.

Once the method is familiar, apply it to a quality you need to develop. Remember you already have this virtue and are really reawakening it. Use the technique of visualising the quality in someone else, then experiencing it for yourself. Always include the phases of imagining its use, the awareness of when it is used through the day, and of evening review.

Never be disappointed in yourself. See a 'failure' as an opportunity to learn.

Never be disappointed in yourself. See a 'failure' as an opportunity to learn. You will be amazed at how quickly this attention improves the quality of your daily life.

Always be positive, appreciate yourself, find and absorb the virtues of others and enjoy developing a new way of living.

THIRTEEN

Spiritual Effort: Positive Thoughts and Attitudes

The best diet for meditation is to feed positive thoughts and feelings to the mind. Making effort to maintain a positive attitude is a feature of the journey of realisation. It is also a feature of lesser worldly ideals, such as acquiring wealth or staying healthy. In view of this application to the limited desires of body-consciousness, I feel that positive attitude has lost its meaning and purpose.

Veronica, a special person from my clinical experience, developed metastatic melanoma in her late thirties. What began for her as a limited desire to beat cancer became a much greater adventure. When Veronica was told that she would die from the condition, she reacted at first with shock and disbelief, and then with determination. Strong willed, she was not going to accept this prognosis. She had too much to live for: a loving husband, two adolescent daughters, a good job and an extended network of friends and relatives rallying behind her.

She elected to fight, believing that she could beat cancer with a positive attitude and an altered lifestyle. Veronica and her husband David attended a retreat with a group of other cancer patients and their partners. The result was wonderful and completely satisfying. They learnt about complementary approaches, including diet, meditation and 'attitudinal healing', whilst developing supportive bonds with others who believed in the potential for cure. Veronica left with the conviction that she could heal herself and was now armed with the knowledge, skills and techniques to do so.

Everyone agreed that Veronica had an extremely positive attitude. Her intelligence, balance and energy drew tremendous support from friends, relatives and connections. The congregation of her local church prayed for her healing, while David was a wonderful support. He took on new domestic duties, juiced fruits and vegetables for her 'anti-cancer' diet and created spaces for Veronica to meditate. Despite this there was a visible, relentless progression of secondary cancers, which were growing beneath the skin where she could see and feel them. For about a year they grew slowly and painlessly, without affecting her function or vitality. She felt good and maintained the strong conviction that any day, just around the corner, they would simply dissolve away. She never entertained the possibility of failure.

In the two months before I met her, the tumours had grown much more rapidly. She also lost her appetite and experienced a reduction in her energy and well-being. On account of increasing pain and loss of sleep, she had become uncharacteristically irritable with her family. Through all of this she never once considered that she would die of cancer.

As the pain got worse, simple pain-killers no longer helped and Veronica's local doctor persuaded her to try morphine. On our first consultation the following day, she was in complete despair. Though pain-free, she was devastated. As soon as I sat her down in the consulting room, she burst into tears. Not just ordinary crying, but the sobbing of hopelessness and failure.

Sitting beside her, David looked helpless and apologetic.

To his credit he didn't say anything but understood a need was being met. Confronted by Veronica's conviction in healing he had bottled up the feeling that they were losing the battle.

As the sobbing subsided, I encouraged her to tell me where it had come from.

'The morphine,' she said.

'The morphine?'

'Yes, the morphine!' Her voice was angry now. 'It means that I have failed. Failed, failed, failed …!' On the fringe of losing control again, she made a huge effort and composed herself. 'Up until today, I have never, not even for a moment, thought I could die. Now I know the situation is hopeless … completely hopeless.'

Desperation overshadowed her resignation. I hesitated, unsure of the best response then said, 'Veronica, I need to know all about this situation. Let's go back. Back to when you first noted a problem with your health. Do you feel you can go over this with me now?' She nodded, actually grateful to leave her present predicament for a while. She went on to tell me the whole story, including their attendance at the retreat and her endeavour to beat cancer. She told me about her discipline with the anti-cancer diet, about her meditation and her faith, of how her church was praying for her, and of how good everyone had been to her.

She was much calmer as we returned to the present. I continued, 'Veronica, it seems to me that starting morphine was the final straw. The tumours kept growing, while your weight, energy and vitality were all deteriorating. Yet you maintained the conviction that you would be healed. With great determination you even withstood two months of severe pain but when you started the morphine it all hit home. Nothing had prepared you for the shock of realising that nothing had worked.'

'Yes. But it's more than that. I feel as if I have failed.'

'In what way?'

'I feel as if I have failed everyone. David and the girls; they've given so much support and commitment to my recovery. Now I've let them down. All my friends, everybody who has been good to me. Everybody who has been praying for my recovery.'

A solitary tear rolled down David's cheek as she continued, 'If only I'd tried harder. Tried harder for everyone. If only my faith were stronger. I'm just not good enough. Now I've made everyone's life miserable. I feel so ... so helpless. And so worthless. It's like everything I've been doing for the last year was for nothing.' She paused, apparently finished.

I asked quietly. 'Has anything positive come out of your cancer experience?'

Wiping her eyes, she looked surprised and thought for a moment. 'Well, yes,' she began. 'My daughter is much closer to me now. We used to fight but she's been fantastic. It's as if she's grown up. She's so sensitive and considerate now. And David ...' she glanced in his direction, their eyes meeting in love and appreciation. 'Our relationship wasn't really the best before I was diagnosed. But he's been wonderful, and we've grown really close again. It's been lovely.'

'I really appreciate life now. A sunrise, a bird singing, a moment of intimacy. My values have changed and I've grown a lot.'

'So it's drawn the whole family together,' I said.

She considered this for a moment, then said, 'And I've changed. I've become much easier going. The things I used to worry about just pass me by now. I'm not so bothered by what people think. It's just great to be alive each day. I really appreciate life now. A sunrise, a bird singing, a moment of intimacy. My values have changed and I've grown a lot.'

She sparkled as another idea occurred to her. 'And

David's changed too. He's contented with simpler things, not so materially driven and much more giving as a person. We've both grown through the last year. More so, perhaps, than we could have done in a whole lifetime without the cancer.'

Enjoying herself now, Veronica continued. 'And another thing, I've really felt close to God in the last twelve months. I've always had faith as a Catholic, but now I really feel like I have a *relationship* with God. It's as if Jesus has walked into my life, and is showing me new and wonderful things.'

As she stopped speaking on this note, Veronica seemed peaceful. Reassured. There was not a trace of the sorrow she had been experiencing only a few moments ago. As she looked at me, I felt it was my turn to speak.

'Veronica, I feel that everything you've done in the last year has been a success. The disease has progressed, and yes, it is catching up with you. But there has been so much growth and transition for you all.' I spent the next few minutes affirming the value of all her efforts. 'You have strengthened your will through discipline, diet and life-style changes. You have become more peaceful and contented through your meditation. Your attitude has both supported and guided your family. And you have realised the true declaration of faith to be in a *relationship* with God.'

After a pause I continued, 'But you were so focused on making the cancer go away, that you didn't notice these things. By making the cancer a yardstick of success or failure, you didn't fully appreciate the meaning of healing.

'I believe that a disease may come to make us grow in some way. Cancer can move you along spiritually, with or without your awareness. You have experienced healing in spite of the relentless progression of your cancer. So continue what you have been doing. Relax the diet, perhaps, to relieve pressure. But do everything now with more balanced objectives between spiritual and physical healing. By all means remain hopeful of remission but let this be a bonus.

'Your healing can continue even if the disease progresses. If you have to die young it is worth realising that few elderly people achieve what you have. The benefits of your growth and spiritual knowledge will influence your family. You will continue to model and shape their lives, even when you are no longer here for them.'

Sitting together we all felt somehow connected and uplifted. Veronica was euphoric. She had come in a state of despair and devastation. She had felt a complete failure. During the consultation, we discovered that her yardstick of success or failure had been whether or not she died of cancer. A reorientation towards spiritual objectives had given her another way of looking at healing, and her entire philosophy had been validated.

Veronica subsequently let go of her fear of death and her spirituality enriched everyone before she 'left'. She personifies the value of including spiritual objectives whenever we aim to be positive.

Thoughts are the seeds of what we experience. If we could train the mind to think only positive thoughts then we would experience life accordingly. When Veronica was diagnosed she set out with the thought, 'I can beat cancer.' For twelve months she was radiantly positive despite having a concealed fear of dying. Morphine unveiled this fear when the thought of the cancer winning brought overwhelming despair. When Veronica replaced her mortal attitude of failure with the thought, 'I am a soul fulfilling the spiritual purpose of my life,' she experienced deep joy, satisfaction and acceptance. Nothing had changed except that her attitude now reflected spiritual immortality, and she was free from the limited aim of staying healthy.

This reflects the main effort needed to sustain a positive attitude, which is to remember and affirm that, 'I am a soul, fulfilling the spiritual purpose of my life'. This also involves an endeavour to express ourselves according to such awareness at all times, under all circumstances.

FOURTEEN

Meditation Exercises: Becoming Positive

*P*ositive thoughts, words and actions benefit others, make us feel good and create a good atmosphere. Negative thoughts, words and actions have the opposite effects. They hurt others and spoil the atmosphere.

Selecting what we do represents a function of the intellect, which is a filter between thinking (the mind) and acting (the body). The intellect 'governs' the mind through its capacity to discern, to judge and to decide. A positive attitude emerges when we use the intellect to express spiritual purpose in thoughts, words, actions and relationships.

First discern truth from falsehood, then judge what conforms to spiritually right action, before deciding how to act. Training oneself to discern, judge and act in this way expresses spirituality. Truly positive people are revealed when their decisions consistently result in three principal outcomes:

- They remain contented and bring peace, happiness and contentment to others.
- They cooperate and thereby make others cooperative.
- They promote spiritual awareness on the basis of their personality and actions.

When we apply ourselves to these aims we are able to valuate our progress. By observing the results of our words and actions, we can review the quality of our decision-making and judgement: 'Did I bring about peace, co-operation or spiritual awareness?' If we make mistakes we learn from them and strengthen our minds. In this way we see that our mistakes have a purpose rather than believing that we are failing.

Even with a spiritual attitude, it may be difficult to conform in our actions. There is a reason for this. Actions are also influenced by our nature and personality, which include the following three obstacles to spiritual progression:

• acquired habits, dependencies and personality traits;
• self-centredness; and
• prejudice.

Latent within us is an original, pure personality, which has been gradually conditioned through life-experiences. What evolves are habitual patterns, dependencies, ego and prejudice, which begin to override the intellect on how we think and behave. Our ability to discern, judge, decide and act spiritually weakens, and con-ditioning ultimately influences the expression of the soul. The effort to become positive is one of renewing the dominance of intellect over conditioning, and one of re-awakening soul-consciousness.

Beginning with the thought, 'I am a soul, fulfilling the spiritual purpose of my life,' we can focus and strengthen the intellect.

Beginning with the thought, 'I am a soul, fulfilling the spiritual purpose of my life,' we can focus and strengthen the intellect. At the same time we exercise control over our prejudices, and over the habit of seeing weaknesses in others. To achieve this we must first become observers of our own attitudes and actions, then endeavour to bring peace, cooperation and truth into the world. In effect we become peaceful and develop a nature of love and simplicity, which is not influenced by the negativity of others.

Exercise 1: Affirming True Identity and Purpose

Enter meditation in the same way as outlined in Chapter 12. Once you are in meditation, affirm to yourself, 'I am a peaceful soul (spirit, light energy, eternal being), fulfilling the spiritual purpose of my life.' Make these positive thoughts of identity and purpose firm. They are quiet internal affirmations of love for your true self. Repeat them in your mind, then pause into lengthy silences and let yourself experience the positive feelings and emotions they bring.

Spend ten to fifteen minutes with this exercise at the beginning of the day, then one to two minutes, every two hours throughout the day, and finally ten minutes before bed at night. Be disciplined initially and you will find it becomes a pleasure. Pleasure makes it habit-forming, so that it transforms from a disciplined to a desirable activity.

Exercise 2: Observing the Mind

This exercise is conducted throughout the waking hours. It involves self-control, internal review and preparation for confronting circumstances. The aim is to remain positive in actions, and to be aware of negative thoughts or emotions.

Holding onto the affirmations of Exercise 1, determine to have positive thoughts for yourself and others. Observe the effects of your words and actions throughout the day. Evaluate or discern whether they bring about one of our three aims — to make others more peaceful, happy or contented; to bring about cooperation; or to create self-awareness.

Initially this discernment may follow an event, when you realise that you acted without thinking. According to your nature or habits you may have reacted to something under the influence of arrogance, anger or selfish desire. Try to be aware of the feelings you have after performing right or wrong actions but be an observer. Remember you are trying to gradually correct rather than punish yourself. As the first step you are coming to know your own mind better.

Recognise, in particular, when you have used discernment, judgement and decision-making effectively. Progressively you will find greater consistency in being positive, as the intellect strengthens its control over your actions.

Be aware in advance of what you might need in a confronting situation and prepare yourself for it. In particular 'arm' yourself with virtues, such as tolerance, patience and respect for the self and others. This will prevent you from coming under the influence of strong personal desires for a particular outcome, and keep you centred on being spiritual.

As you knowingly use the powers of the intellect, and connect with your virtues, you find others become cooperative. Not immediately perhaps, but in time. Eventually, through this training of the mind, you will automatically respond to situations correctly. You will not have to go through preparation. The training actually makes you *ever-ready* such that, when conflict comes without warning, you are completely stable, unaffected and accurate.

As part of this retraining of the mind, I recommend daily review of how positive you have been. It is useful to keep a written chart or diary to this end, which will give you a record of progress over time. Always consider 'failures' to have been lessons whose purpose is to make you stronger.

Review what happened. Were you weak in discernment, judgement or decision-making? Did you come under the influence of fear, old habits or a personality trait? Did you react under the influence of greed, anger or ego? Did you feel compelled to carry out an action even though you had discerned it to be hurtful? Consider the influence behind the compulsion, for this is a habit you can change through your awareness of it.

Maintain a positive and nurturing approach to yourself. Concentrate on your effectiveness and increase your awareness when there are 'failures'. If you turn an obstacle into a learning experience in this way, then you have successfully transformed it to love.

FIFTEEN

Spiritual Effort: Eliminating Waste and Negativity

Waste and negativity begin with a thought that is either useless or vindictive. The experience created actually separates us from love. Wasteful patterns are harmless but serve no purpose. Thinking about situations and people you can't change, worrying about the future, or wishing that you could change the past. Why waste time and energy thinking or talking about the actions or attitudes of others? The term negativity relates to vindictive or hurtful thoughts, words or actions, which cause suffering in the self or others.

In the last two chapters we looked at the important effort of *being* positive. We also considered how life-experience conditions our nature and attitudes. In effect we were looking at the whole energy that now defines our consciousness. It is the capacity to think, to decide, to express and to record memories or experiences.

This defines the self as a living, conscious energy, which acts through the body. I have, on occasion, had a distinct sense of 'presence' whilst examining a body immediately after death. I have felt that the one who recently left was still intact and close by. It has led me to believing that everything that defines personality is in the soul. Certainly it is not in the bodies I examine. Whatever was living has gone and is still living.

In 1992 I encountered Raja Yoga meditation and its philosophy of the soul. It felt like I had stumbled on something that was accurate and simple. Essentially it goes like this: 'I am a soul and not a body, my original nature was peace and everything experienced or expressed is a faculty of the soul.' According to Raja Yoga, a soul or spirit contains three aspects of consciousness, namely: the conscious mind; the intellect; and the *sanskaras* (subconscious mind, nature or personality).

Sanskara is an Eastern term, which relates to an impression or imprint left on the soul by a past action or experience. The original nature of a soul is pure and innocent, before it develops the sanskaras of negative encounters. Under the influence of these, the soul itself develops a capacity for fear, impure thoughts, tendencies or feelings. As it becomes body-conscious, wasteful and negative patterns emerge.

These sanskaras condition and change our personalities. As they accumulate they affect the soul like rust on a shiny needle, hiding its original purity and sparkle. The effort-making required to eliminate waste and negativity is about removing this 'rust' and rediscovering our original purity.

Now imagine the mind as a garden where wasteful thoughts and negativity are weeds; left untended these overgrow and choke all that is beautiful. Wise gardeners cultivate the beauty of a garden, with flowers and plants that prevent weeds from growing. They then keep it under constant surveillance, removing the occasional weed before it becomes established. More careless gardeners allow the garden to become overgrown, then spend two thankless days of labour pulling out the weeds. After experiencing satisfaction for a few days, they let it get out of hand again, and the cycle repeats.

The spiritual aspirant could be viewed in this way. As a gardener of the mind, he or she would be wise to cultivate beauty and balance. Weeds are controlled under a 'ground-cover' of stability, tolerance and patience, while the seeds of virtue are planted to make the 'garden' bloom. Through regular careful surveillance, wasteful or negative thoughts are pruned before they come into expression.

In the previous chapters we considered the spiritual efforts of appreciation and positive attitudes. From the 'garden' of the mind we can see that these efforts contribute to the elimination of waste and negativity. In this chapter, we will now focus on transforming wasteful thoughts and negativity through spiritual detachment and responsibility. Spiritual detachment does not mean distancing ourselves or becoming coldly dissociated from others. On the contrary it reflects a sense of self that is neither influenced by the negativity of others, nor affected by circumstances that would otherwise have caused distress, fear or reactivity. By looking through the 'eyes' of self-knowledge, we understand that people act under the influence of body-consciousness; and it is their body-consciousness that we try to detach from.

Consider my work with the terminally ill, where I come into intimate relationship with people facing death, loss and separation from all that they love. In my role as a physician I can offer much needed help with pain control but I also try to enter each such relationship with spiritual awareness. When I succeed in this I find that I am lighter, more relaxed and attentive, and more responsive to their suffering.

Through self-awareness I automatically sense the eternal nature of others and witness suffering as a temporary phase of spiritual adjustment. This brings a feeling of closeness and empathy, without being distressed or reactive. I find that people will then 'open up', so that I can understand their physical, emotional or spiritual needs more deeply.

So spiritual awareness brings detachment from suffering yet leads to a warmer, closer and more loving relationship.

Whatever the beliefs of someone frightened by death, they will be comforted by the company of faith, that is, by the presence of quiet spiritual awareness. Such presence is an expression in itself that all is well in destiny; you need not even say a word. To be detached in this way allows you to see others as they are, and enables you to discern their needs appropriately.

When it is a projection of spiritual awareness, detachment enables us to become non-judgemental observers. By understanding that vindictive attitudes come from body-consciousness, we develop a merciful outlook in which we accept people as they are. Except through example there is no need to interfere with the attitudes or destiny of others, and no need to waste time contemplating negative thoughts about them.

With such acceptance, trust and understanding, we can develop a profound state of self-respect. This enables us to face our weaknesses without feeling hurt or angry when someone faults our words or actions. Some years ago, when working as a palliative care registrar, I was asked to see the wife of a retired medical colleague. She had advanced bowel cancer, with secondary spread to the liver. As she was too unwell to come to the hospital, I arranged to visit them at home. My colleague met me at the door and asked to speak to me for a few minutes first. He told me that he had kept the knowledge of cancer from her, and asked me not to discuss it with her.

The consultation went well. She didn't seem to want to know and I was effective in relieving her pain. Several weeks later I was called again. There had been a considerable deterioration, and she was troubled by constant nausea. When I arrived at the home, I could see that things were pretty desperate. She was severely wasted, bed-bound and deeply jaundiced (yellow, from liver failure).

On this occasion she asked, 'Do you think I will get better?' Remembering she had been kept in the dark, I replied with a question. 'Well, how do things appear to you? How have you been recently?'

'Terrible,' she said. 'I'm sick all the time. I'm getting weaker. And I can hardly do anything for myself ...' She paused. 'So, will I get better?'

Perhaps she was looking for reassurance. I felt she was trying to understand what was happening to her and wanted an honest answer. 'I'm sorry,' I said. 'But I don't think you will get better. There's a bit of a problem with your liver, and I think it's getting worse.'

'How do you know that?' I noticed the anxiety of her voice and body language. As gently as possible I answered, 'There's a tinge of yellow visible in your eyes and skin. It's a sign.' I was being a master of understatement; she was as yellow as a lemon.

Tears rolled down her cheeks. 'I'm going to die, aren't I?'

'I'm sorry but I think you may,' I replied. 'I think it's to do with the old cancer problem. It seems to have flared up a bit, in the liver.'

'What can you do for me?' she asked.

'First of all, I can get rid of this nausea trouble you've been having ...' I went on to assure her that we would be able to deal with any new problems; that she would not suffer from excessive pain; and that we would help her towards a peaceful passage from this life to the next.

A couple of days later, I telephoned to check whether my prescribing had settled the vomiting. It had. But my medical colleague's voice was disapproving. I felt uncomfortable but asked if he would like me to review her progress in a week or so. He said, 'No thank you, Dr Cole. You are no longer welcome here, so goodbye and please don't call again.'

I was stunned and felt like a train had hit me in the pit

of the stomach. Had I been insensitive or, worse still, incompetent? As I went through the rest of the day my mind was unable to function effectively; I couldn't stop going over and over the situation. Intellectually I felt I had done my job but my emotions were in turmoil. She asked for honesty and I responded in a necessary way. She needed to know, otherwise how could she understand why life was so bad for her?

Hurt and full of self-doubt I went straight to the ward, needing to successfully relieve someone's suffering and to have that recognised. Despite being seen as someone with relatively high self-esteem, I needed to be validated. I needed to hear a patient tell me that I was wonderful, and that I had made everything much clearer. I needed to have someone's regard or admiration.

If I had possessed greater self-respect, the phone call would not have influenced me. Self-respect, or the deep acceptance of self, is a form of humility that expresses automatic regard for everyone. Had I possessed this I would have been firm in my feeling that I had done the best I could. Even if I had made a mistake, I would have seen this as an opportunity to learn rather than experience despair. When there is self-respect and humility there is no room for waste or negativity.

When there is self-respect and humility there is no room for waste or negativity.

I have so far considered that spiritual detachment means to possess a strong sense of self, which is not influenced by the negativity of others. It is a way of loving others as eternal beings and of understanding that they too have been deceived by body-consciousness.

To consider that everything resides within a divine plan is the final aspect of spiritual detachment I would like to address. Consider for a moment that the world is a huge stage where each soul has a unique and accurate part to play. An actor plays his own part without concern for the roles of others. Concentrating on his own role he simply observes and interacts with the roles of others, never trying to take on their parts. You can become an observer of the drama of life in this way. I believe we live in a complex age but have the conviction that it is a benevolent drama, even when the scenes contain suffering or pain. With a spiritual attitude imagine you are sitting in a cinema being entertained by each scene. Through soul-consciousness you see everything differently and understand that immortality leaves no room for worry, fear or concern. A sense of higher purpose prevents wasteful or negative thoughts and feelings from emerging.

The second aspect of eliminating waste and negativity is that of taking responsibility. I recently spoke with a meditation teacher who was lamenting an error with two students. They had been attending a group programme run by my friend. They were really interested in the philosophy expressed, and wanted to experience peace and positivity in their lives. They committed themselves to a five-week course in meditation. As a couple, they seemed enthusiastic, but turned up late on the first night. They did so again on the second, disrupting the group with a lame excuse. After the session my friend confronted them. She told them that they would only find peace, and a positive attitude, if they took more responsibility for themselves. They never returned.

My friend felt that she had been too hard on them and had offended them. There may have been some truth in this, but it also demonstrates a limitation common to the world today. Many people who are drawn toward peace and spirituality, are unwilling to *be* responsible for themselves. Once they find that it can't be done for them, and that they have to engage disciplines to change themselves, they lose interest. People want peace, and they want a quick fix in a quick-fix society. They also want to blame others for their 'peace-lessness', saying things like:

'I got angry because so and so said ...'

'It's not my fault.'

'They made me do it.'

Until we begin to be responsible for our actions, our feelings and responses, we will continue to be the victims of our circumstances. When we become responsible, and cease to blame, we are engaging the efforts of self-transformation. Instead of blaming after a bout of anger it is better that we take responsibility, resolve to change and thereby increase our power of tolerance. Such responsibility brings greater self-control and is an act of love, which nurtures growth.

SIXTEEN

Meditation Exercise: Spiritual Detachment

This can be used concurrently with the other exercises we have covered. Together they offer a variety of ways to focus on different yet related aspects of spiritual growth. What I hope to demonstrate is that growth is a disciplined, constant self-training process. With the variety on offer through these exercises, I hope the reader will find refreshing ways to experiment with self-realisation.

As with the previous meditation exercises there are three components:

- meditation;
- discernment through the day;
- review.

In the first part we will focus on self-respect and accepting others. Enter meditation as outlined previously. Once you have relaxed for ten minutes or so, let someone enter your mind. Someone you have difficulty with. Perhaps not the most difficult person in your life as it might be a bit hard to start there! Maybe someone you like to avoid, or someone you react to when you see them coming. The sort of person you hope didn't see you when you pretended not to notice them. Or someone who takes up your time and seems oblivious to your needs.

You have an established pattern of relating to this individual, and this is common to all of us. We categorise souls, putting them into boxes, labelled: friend; foe; associate; annoying; arrogant; stupid; good; bad and so on. We react immediately to them in accordance with these labels. Once categorised we tend to keep them there, with the lid firmly closed on those we dislike. To accept people as they are, we need first to remove the labels and let them out of the boxes. Second, we must acquire the habit of not labelling people altogether.

Now visualise or imagine your person to be in a box, with the lid on. Take a look at the box in your mind. See if you can see the label you have on it. Then think to yourself, 'If I let you go, you can be yourself, and I can also be free in our relationship.'

Now imagine yourself removing the label. Do so with the merciful thought, 'You are only like this because there have been losses in your life. I understand now, that you have forgotten who you are.'

Allow this awareness to create the feeling that you should free this person from your box. Don't open the lid unless this feeling and the awareness are well developed. Once the feeling is well cultivated, open the box and imagine that the person is happy and liberated from the prison of your mind.

'I know you now as a soul. You are a traveller like me. Farewell, my friend.'

As they appear happy, accept them completely with this thought, 'I know you now as a soul. You are a traveller like me. Farewell, my friend.'

Let them go from your mind, then review how it felt to do so. It is a good feeling. Within it you experience greater self-respect, having overcome a weakness in yourself that had made you body-conscious toward the nature of another.

This exercise makes you more soul-conscious, as you

forgive someone's behaviour by understanding that it has been conditioned by sorrow. Work on one person at a time and you will witness remarkable results. Relationships will change. You will stop reacting in the predetermined way, having freed yourself from being so affected. Those people will also respond to you in a more satisfactory way. Having done this exercise earnestly with a few people, something remarkable happens. Your habit of labelling people ends and you become tolerant of the way people are.

In a way these labels have 'protected' you from feeling vulnerable, upset or angry. As you let them go, you are really letting go of your own fear and *learning how to love*. You learn to accept people as they are and become non-judgemental. With greater wisdom and understanding, it automatically follows that your self-respect deepens. This in turn strengthens you in the face of criticism, and enables you to become stable in fluctuating circumstances.

In association with this meditation exercise, tackle the day as an observer of the drama. See everything that happens as 'meant to be' or as a lesson. Remember that you serve others through detachment, which promotes peace and contentment. As you learn to detach and observe, you will become more spiritually discerning. Wiser and more accurate. Knowing when to speak and when to keep quiet. You will come to understand people better. And with this knowledge, you will learn how to support people that they may grow.

Become an observer when you are criticised or praised. Respond appropriately but allow a sense of detachment to leave you less affected. It is easier in the beginning to control your reaction to praise. As you achieve this, self-respect grows automatic (not needing regard from others) and you find yourself less affected by criticism.

As an observer you are keeping yourself under review and developing a stage of being introverted. This is a means of moving towards wisdom and self-control. Review the day internally and learn the lessons of 'failures' by seeing them as the hidden facilitators of growth. Remember that when you are making effort there must be 'failure' along the way. Otherwise no effort would be required!

SEVENTEEN

Spiritual Effort: Letting Go

In Chapter 5 we looked at an example of acceptance before Margaret died of cancer. By letting go completely, accepting her destiny and yielding to circumstance she became the embodiment of love and surrender. Through the use of meditation we can apply this lesson from the dying and discover how to surrender. In Raja Yoga this is termed 'dying alive', which really means dying to our old nature through self-realisation. The spiritual effort of letting go is the key to this process.

At forty-seven Maria was relatively young to be dying of cervical cancer. She was a slightly built Chinese Buddhist, who had a husband and two children, aged ten and fourteen. She had presented three years earlier with vaginal bleeding from a small cancer of the cervix. Following a hysterectomy she remained well, put the cancer experience behind her and returned to a normal lifestyle.

Two months before being transferred to my care she had a recurrence of cancer in the pelvis. It was extensive, involving the bladder, rectum and pelvic side-wall. Though incurable, a surgeon offered aggressive treatment, in which he operated and removed all that he could including the rectum and bladder. Maria was left with a colostomy bag for faeces and a second bag, an ileal-conduit, for urine drainage. Both bags were on the front of her stomach. She was given six weeks of post-operative radiotherapy.

She never really recovered from this. She progressively lost weight, energy and well-being, and never returned to work. When she arrived in the hospice she was withdrawn, very depressed, in severe pain and surrounded by an offensive odour, with bags containing bodily waste on her abdomen. We initially relieved her pain and started her on antibiotics to reduce the odour.

I subsequently visited her twice a week. She was in a miserable, despairing, hopeless state of mind. Each time I asked how she was feeling, she replied, 'I can't bear this. I don't want to live any more. Please end it for me now.' From time to time people make such requests. Generally it's more a way of expressing hopelessness than a genuine request for euthanasia. In Maria's case it was both genuine and firm; she definitely wanted me to end her life and looked at me with expectation. On each visit I asked her why it was so unbearable that she wanted to die.

She replied, 'I'm so disgusting.' She couldn't bear to look at the bags on her abdomen. 'I'm useless, worthless and there's no point to my life. I have no energy, I can't do anything, I'm not a woman and I hate myself. No-one can help me.' When I asked her how this made her feel, she said, 'So unhappy, so unhappy,' then started to cry. She told me that she couldn't bear seeing her husband and children because they reminded her of how happy she had once been, and she felt jealous that they were well. Talking to her family, I discovered that her husband was feeling really helpless and that her children were grieving and feeling rejected. On each visit I first listened to her feelings and perspectives before telling her that it was both illegal and against my spiritual beliefs to end her life. She accepted this, saying that she had appreciated the opportunity to talk it over.

For six weeks we had exactly the same discussion, twice a

week. It seemed that she needed to keep expressing it. During this period we arranged for her to have weekend leave, and go home with her family. To our disappointment it was a disaster. We had hoped it would make her feel better and help to rebuild her relationships. On the contrary she returned more depressed and had distanced herself further from her children. They were in an emotional turmoil. On the plus side, Maria and I had developed a good rel-ationship and her depression had been lightening. It was at this time that I explored her spiritual beliefs. She seemed happier after talking about her religion and agreed to a pastoral visit from a Buddhist monk.

Over the next two weeks she became happy and stopped requesting euthanasia. She said that she felt contented and ready to die when it was her time. Much to their relief she now welcomed her husband and children. Instead of the previous tension and withdrawal, we would find them with their arms around each other, beaming with happiness.

On one of my visits I asked her how the monk had made such a difference. 'He told me that disease is a result of past karma (actions),' she said, 'and that I had to accept it. He said it was a cleansing process, which was preparing me for spiritual ascendancy in my next birth.' Maria continued, 'I now understand that I am settling some old karmic accounts, which is part of becoming a free spirit.' I was relieved by this development. Through finding meaning, her anger and sorrow had dispersed. She now had a purpose and spiritual 'knowledge' had given her self-respect.

She continued, 'He said that the greater my equanimity, the less my spirit would struggle before taking rebirth. He told me to stop making my family suffer. He made me see that I would stop feeling disgusting to them by not feeling disgusted with myself.'

He went on to talk to her of the Buddhist philosophy of impermanence. Everything changes, nothing stays the same. Suffering results from trying to hold on to what must change. Individual life, he said, is a series of changing relationships through different births. We might meet again at different times but never in the same way. Everything we have is impermanent and temporary, yet we hold on to everything for security or happiness and live in fear of loss. We become trapped in a web of attachments where loss is inevitable because nothing can remain the same.

Everything changes, nothing stays the same. Suffering results from trying to hold on to what must change.

'He told me to let go,' Maria said. 'To let go of all my attachments, which he said was the true road to freedom and happiness. So I have been doing this, letting go of my attachment to health; to the things I used to enjoy doing; to my family; and to the future that I expected to have. Once he put it all in perspective for me, it became easy. I've never felt freer or happier than I do now.' Maria lived for another three weeks before stepping peacefully into the afterlife. With her Buddhist counsellor present, she left her body without anxiety, concern or agitation.

Attachments are developed because we need security, comfort and happiness. Wherever there is attachment there is also dependence. This makes it very challenging to let go, so it is important to know what we are letting go of. In *The Tibetan Book of Living and Dying* (Random House, 1994), Sogyal Rinpoche gives a beautiful example of its meaning. Consider, for a moment, that your hand is closed tightly around a coin. If you stretch out your arm and let go of the coin, palm down, it falls to the ground and you lose it. If you do the same thing with your palm facing up, you let it go yet it remains with you.

In the same way, letting go does not mean having to lose something. It is not our actual health, wealth or relationships that we let go of, it is being dependent on them. Dependency is an aspect of ego and body-consciousness, while letting go is an aspect of becoming soul-conscious. Being able to free ourselves from dependency begins when we recognise our spirit, and have faith in our immortality. Like clouds that obscure sunlight, attachment and dependency bring temporary happiness but keep us in the shadow of spiritual ignorance. When we let go we emerge from the shadows and see the light.

Letting go also means to stop being affected by what happened in the past, or concerned about what might happen in the future. This can be very challenging for those who have been hurt badly, or for those who are faced with uncertainty. To be free from the past we need to forgive, and to be free from the future we need to trust.

I couldn't recount the number of times I have heard a patient or family member say, 'I will never forgive … and I will never forget.' Yet the memory they choose to hold on to is causing them sorrow and anger. They are still suffering from the past and seem unable to find reconciliation or peace. It's a great challenge to forgive people who have traumatised us. In the first instance we may feel that they don't deserve to be forgiven. Yet, unless we forgive, we can't forget. And, unless we forget, we can't free ourselves from their influence. In a sense they still have us trapped from the distance.

Perhaps we could start with the question, 'Do I deserve to be free from that person or situation?' The answer of course is, 'Yes, because I was innocent.' Forgiveness is really an attitude that frees the self and enables us to forget. It doesn't need to be spoken or written unless you find this helps. Although it may not affect or change those that hurt you, it finishes their ongoing power over your well-being. In the strangest of ways, if you learn this lesson, then the person who hurt you has made you stronger.

To be free from guilt we sometimes need to forgive ourselves. Although we can't change what we did we can resolve to learn from the mistake. Forgive yourself and let go but don't forget. The memory will caution and prevent you from acting wrongly again. By turning mistakes into learning, forgiveness develops within us an attitude that is loving and non-judgemental. This, in turn, enables our love to flow effortlessly to others.

To live in the moment we must trust in the future and let go of expectations, worry or concern about how things might turn out. Let go of needing things to work out for you. By all means make plans, then live in the present and let the future come to you. By trusting in whatever happens is to be unconditional, unattached and free from dependency. Try to see that everything is in divine order and that when things go wrong they were meant to. Sometimes this requires complete faith in the spiritual dimension, in the temporary nature of suffering, and in some form of creative higher power. Trust brings us closer to the liberated, free and happy state of mind that characterises acceptance.

The spiritual effort of letting go is a progressive surrender of ego, which leads to one final subtle thread of attachment. This final trace of arrogance or body-consciousness is the consciousness of 'I' or 'mine', reflecting possessiveness or the desire for regard and recognition.

'What did you say about my daughter?'

'I should have been consulted.'

'That's mine, leave it alone.'

'I did it.'

The subtlety of this consciousness is deceptive. Even with substantial surrender, the desire for your name to be known or for someone to speak highly of you can persist. It is a delicate veil that we may not recognise, yet it deceives us and leads us away from all that is divine.

A method to free yourself from this final aspect of attachment is to consider yourself a trustee of possessions and relationships, whilst living as a 'guest' in this world.

EIGHTEEN

Meditation Exercise: Being a Trustee and a Guest

I n this exercise we will endeavour to cultivate the habit of being a trustee and a guest in this world. Nothing belongs to a trustee and a guest always has good and respectful manners. When something is loaned, rather than owned, it is taken better care of and used properly. We will experiment with the idea that everything 'I' have, in terms of my body, wealth, possessions and relationships, really belongs to the divine. Instead of owning these things I have been entrusted with them to use on behalf of the divine. We will also experiment with the idea that, wherever 'I' am, I am a guest in the 'household' of the divine, behaving with divinity.

What you relate to as 'the divine' is up to you. For me it is God, who I see as a radiant point of light, love, knowledge and purity, who resides beyond our universe yet relates like a mother, father, friend and teacher. For you the form and location of the divine may differ from my reference. If you don't believe in an external manifestation then look to the divine within the self. At least you know that you exist so consider the divine to be your 'higher self'. For the purpose of this exercise I will refer to 'the divine', and leave the interpretation to you.

See everything you have as belonging to the divine; as a trustee become an instrument, using whatever you have to spread the influence of spirituality through pure feelings and good wishes; as a guest become a welcome and influential observer of the scenes of drama. As for previous exercises, begin with morning meditation, pay attention throughout the day, and review your process at night.

Sitting in a comfortable position, enter meditation as previously described. Relax, let your attention go to the body and develop this awareness of letting go: 'This body is a vehicle on loan from the divine. I am a trustee of this body and a guest in this world.'

Sit in this state of awareness until it feels firm. If you prefer, use some other words, symbols or images of your own. Then extend the idea to all your possessions:

> Nothing belongs to me. Everything I have belongs to the divine, and has been given for the purpose of service. Whatever I have is to bring peace or happiness. I am a guest even of my own household.

Next extend it to your roles. Let all your roles unfold in front of you. Sometimes you are a parent, sometimes a child, sometimes a spouse, sometimes in the role of your job or profession, sometimes a home-maker. Let go of all these roles with the thought:

> These roles belong to the body and the responsibilities belong to the divine. As a trustee, living as a guest amongst spiritual brothers and sisters, I play my part. The divine uses everything I do, to reach everyone I know.

Let the world appear in your mind's eye, like a huge stage on which an enormous drama is being enacted. Whilst a trustee of your body, amidst the influences of your life, you are a guest here also. The divine is the writer and director of the drama, and you are playing your part. You are a guest of the divine, and a guest in the drama. Detached and peaceful, you let the scenes of the world-play entertain you.

There is nothing you have to do except surrender within an accurate and divine drama.

Allow yourself to experience that all responsibilities belong to the divine, and that your only responsibility is to stay within divine influence. Consider all others to be children of the divine who, like you, are guests in the drama, playing their unique and individual roles. No one belongs to you. In life you may be playing the role of a mother or a father but your child is also a soul so is really your 'brother' or 'sister'. And like you that soul is a child and a guest here. Let go of any feelings of possessiveness. No one belongs to you. You may have been entrusted with their care. So be loving as an instrument of the divine.

There is nothing you have to do except surrender within an accurate and divine drama.

Throughout the day take this attitude with you. Nothing is mine. I am playing a part in a divine plan. Nobody belongs to me. Dependency is an illusion, created when I forgot who I belonged to.

Be merciful with these thoughts. Stay detached and loving in the drama of life. Everything is divine. Nothing is wrong. The divine is responsible, and will make everything good with the cooperation of your surrender.

NINETEEN

Spiritual Effort: Maintaining Union with the Divine

Paula is a fifty-one year-old divorcee who will almost certainly have left her body by the time you read this. Diagnosed with metastatic bowel cancer twelve months before I saw her, she resolved not to accept her doctor's prognosis of a few months to live. Determined to beat the disease she sought advice about complementary medicine from a former cancer patient. As a result she changed her lifestyle, took various herbs and adopted a meditation programme.

Like Veronica in Chapter 13, she wouldn't entertain the prospect of failure. Nevertheless, by the time I saw her, she had required two further operations for recurrent disease, followed by a period of increasing pain and weakness. Her quality of life had recently deteriorated and she spoke to her complementary therapist the day before seeing me. They decided that she needed to stop fighting the disease, to accept that she was dying and to have trust in the outcome.

'I could see that I was getting sicker and felt like a failure,' she told me. 'When we looked at why I got cancer, it soon became apparent that I have never really loved myself. I've been a battler and a high achiever, a single mother, a professional and an influential person. I've always been a 'doer' and put others before myself. Despite achieving through my life, I always felt that I was failing in some way or another.' We talked a little about how high achievers are often driven by their fear of failure.

She continued, 'I now need to give in, to surrender and to trust in the divine. I feel so sick, so tired and in so much pain that I'm desperate for relief. That's why I'm turning to you.'

We looked at her symptom control. She had pain in her liver, which was due to secondary cancer as well as low abdominal pain from partial bowel obstruction. When I examined her I found the cause of this to be a mass of cancer blocking most of her rectum. Once I expressed confidence about improving her symptoms she started to talk about her faith.

'I had a strict Catholic upbringing, which left me with a lot of fear and guilt. I used to teach the faith in Sunday school but had to reconcile my religious beliefs when I was divorced, and regretted how dogmatic I'd been. Getting cancer has given me food for thought. Like everything else in my life I've been doing everything because I thought I had to. I've been doing meditation and doing complementary medicine. Frankly, I'm sick of it. What I really want is to love myself, to trust and surrender, and to experience God loving me.'

Expanding on her view of God she told me, 'I'm a bit of a heretic these days but basically still a Catholic. I see God as all that is good within us, and as all that is divine outside of us. If only I could trust in this and surrender enough, I would experience so much love. To me God is like an ocean, which is probably what has motivated me to live by the sea.' Paula had recently moved to the coast. She said, 'As an ocean, God is vast and unlimited. I have been sitting on the beach, opening myself up, trying to feel God's company and relationship. Despite faith since childhood

I've never felt such closeness as I have now. My "busy"-ness, doir.g and achieving have been separating me from experiencing the oneness that is God.'

By talking about her desire for union with the divine, Paula was recognising that the divine is ever-present; and that our own thoughts, words, attitudes and actions connect or separate us from experiencing oneness or union. They can separate us from all the good that is within us, and all that is divine outside of us. I sometimes think that we were once the true children of God but have now become separated like orphans.

I believe there to have been times in my life when I experienced divine union with God. The first occasion following the catharsis I shared in Chapter 4. When we have an experience of union it is both existential and clarifying. It feels like a spiritual window has opened, which, for the first time, enables us to see clearly. However there is a vast difference between attaining and maintaining such union. We can attain the experience of divine union and realise our eternal identity, yet remain body-conscious. Despite the experience we can still be influenced by negative thoughts or feelings, which keep separating us from the divine. It is by control over the direction of our thoughts that we begin to discover how to maintain our spiritual well-being.

In the East there is a saying that our final thoughts lead us to our destination. Gandhi illustrated this as he died at the hands of an assassin, repeating the words, 'Rama, Rama'. His final thoughts were of God (Rama). Although the saying relates to the thoughts we have at the time of death, it is also true of life. The mind travels in the direction of its thoughts. Body-conscious thoughts of waste, negativity, worry or arrogance immediately separate us from the divine. On the other hand, soul-conscious thoughts around our true spiritual identity or the virtues of others bring us into union with the divine.

If we could consistently discern truth from falsehood, then we would always think in a fashion that connects us to the divine. Such thoughts embody peace and love as our constant experience and expression. Everything we perceive through the fabric of body-consciousness is deceptive. Even that which is colourful and attractive can separate us from our divinity.

When souls are no longer misled by body-consciousness, they are able to develop and maintain divine union. I saw this exemplified in 1992, whilst attending an international Raja Yoga meditation retreat, organised by the Brahma Kumaris in India. Their spiritual headquarters resides in the rarefied atmosphere of Mt Abu, overlooking the plains and mountain ranges of Rajasthan. The gentle, contented and peaceful eyes of the resident yogis captivated me. Everyone I met seemed to have them. Divine spiritual eyes that were both surrendered and revealing.

The retreat subsequently demonstrated to me that divine union, soul-consciousness and surrender creates an atmosphere full of love and peace. A sensitive soul entering this atmosphere finds within love a quality that is more than an emotion or a feeling; it is also an intelligent energy that seeds within us the truth of spiritual identity. This has led me to think of divine love as love that has the power to reveal truth.

My original encounter with divine union was one of enlightenment following catharsis. In Mt Abu I discovered that union can also be attained and experienced through meditation. Since then I have been adopting the practices and, progressively, the disciplines of Raja Yoga. Its aim is to attain purity through maintaining union with the divine, which requires effort, awareness, determined thought and discipline.

Divine union purifies in two ways. One is by the direct clearing of negative sanskaras (personality traits) from the soul, while the other involves recognising and realising our original pure sanskaras. It is essentially a process of self-transformation. The sanskaras of negativity affect the soul like rust on a shiny needle. Once corroded, a needle can no longer recognise a magnet or be attracted to it. If you are cleansed of the rust the needle sparkles and, with its magnetism restored, it leaps to the magnet. Likewise a soul, 'corroded' by body-consciousness, neither recognises nor is attracted by the divine. When it becomes enlightened, however, a relationship with the divine can remove the 'rust' and restore the magnetism of purity. Once again, the soul becomes attracted to the divine.

When Paula was describing God, she likened the divine to a vast and unlimited ocean. As souls rediscover the divine, it is as if they are rivers meeting this ocean. By merging into the qualities of the ocean we begin to recognise and realise our own original qualities.

The Ocean of Knowledge invokes our wisdom,
The Ocean of Peace invokes our original nature of peace,
The Ocean of Love invokes our innocence,
The Ocean of Mercy invokes our understanding,
The Ocean of Purity invokes our happiness, and
The Ocean of Forgiveness invokes our freedom.

The divine could be seen in this way, as a vast treasure store of inexhaustible powers and virtues. Through the cleansing of negativity and the invocation of purity, I believe we can become, *once again*, created in the image of the divine. The soul can become pure from impure, soul-conscious from body-conscious; rust-free, sparkling and perfect ... just like the divine.

Two specific disciplines involved with attaining and maintaining union are meditation and remembrance. I learnt about these in Mt Abu and will relate to you my experiences. On one occasion I had been walking along a track leading from the meditation complex around the mountain to a wide ledge. After sitting on the ledge, I took in the breathtaking vista in which mountains rose from the plains of a desert basin, then ambled their way towards the Pakistan border. With eagles gliding serenely beneath me I had about twenty minutes of meditation.

Rising from the ledge I then followed the track in a full circle back to the Mt Abu complex. The ledge eventually gave way to less spectacular terrain and finally a tarred road, which skirted one side of a lake before entering the lively Mt Abu township. By the time I returned, I had walked from the tranquil mountain, through the bustle of the town and back to the serenity of the complex.

As I entered the complex there was music playing, which I barely noticed at first and continued walking. All at once my attention was drawn to the stillness and silence within the compound. Everyone had stopped whatever they were doing and had become motionless. They were standing or sitting silently, conversations frozen mid-sentence.

It was 'traffic control'.

Respectfully I stopped walking, became still and was absorbed into an atmosphere of peace. But there was more than peace. There was something deeper, something greater that I couldn't recognise at first but then understood. It was power. Not the competitive, self-centred power of ego but the benevolent power of spirituality.

This traffic control was conducted for three minutes every two hours, with the aims of maintaining union with the divine and of staying in remembrance. Everyone makes a simultaneous effort to stop the 'traffic' of thoughts and turn the mind to the divine. The result is pure vibrations of love and peace, which unify the complex. One of the yogis explained it to me.

She said, 'God is teaching us here that we are souls. Each one a divine spark of living energy, a tiny point of spiritual light centred in the middle of the forehead.' She pointed to the centre of her forehead and continued. 'We remember this throughout the day, and we stay connected with God, the Supreme Soul, through this remembrance.

'During traffic control we first clear our minds, then share just the one unifying thought of being connected with God.' She paused to let me take this in, then continued. 'This feeling of connection can be achieved in several ways. I often use a personalised approach to experience God in the form of a relationship, such as my Mother, Father, Friend, Companion or Teacher. Whichever one I need at that moment. On other occassions I remember His qualities of purity, mercy, love or forgiveness, and experience these awakening in me. And at other times I simply adopt His form.'

'During traffic control we first clear our minds, then share just the one unifying thought of being connected with God.'

'His form?' I prompted. 'Of a point,' she replied. 'In the form of a soul, God is a point of light, living beyond the material universe. Infinitesimally small, yet, as an ocean of all virtues and powers, God's nature is universal and accessible to all. It makes Him seem omnipresent, like He is everywhere and in everything. Yet His form is only that of a soul, neither male nor female, just a tiny point of spiritual light.'

'How do you know this?' I asked. She chuckled, pointed upwards and said, 'He told us,' before gliding happily away.

When I had understood the object of traffic control, I began to experiment with it for myself. I would open myself, surrender, and find the experience of union to be exquisitely simple. It also resulted in me experiencing a relationship with divinity throughout the day. I gradually learnt more of the yogi lifestyle during my time with them. They were making a sincere and disciplined effort, to surrender completely to God, whilst considering this single act to be one of world service. 'The vibrations of peace reach the whole world from a surrendered soul,' I was told.

The day begins at three-thirty in the morning, when they aim to awaken with the thought that 'I am a child of God.' They then proceed to 'amrit vela', which is the first meditation of the day. In the meditation of Raja Yoga their aim is to attain a union in which the soul 'remembers' God, the divine Mother and Father. So it is meditation, divine union and remembrance. All three.

My yogi friend explained, 'In Raja Yoga meditation we attain a divine union with the Supreme. We call this the seed stage. The highest stage. It is also a beautiful remembrance of our Spiritual Father, and our World Mother. We remember that we are souls, whilst receiving love and power from God. Our aim, throughout the day, is to maintain this connection and consciousness. But it is easy to forget, to become absorbed in our responsibilities, actions or work, and to break our link with God. This is why we have traffic control together. It reminds us to stay in remembrance, to stay connected at all times, whatever we are doing. In this way we are surrendering, and becoming instruments of the divine.'

Everything the yogis do, is done with the spiritual effort to remain in remembrance throughout the day; whether cooking, cleaning or eating. The early morning meditation leads into a day where, ideally, the yoga-link remains unbroken such that remembrance enters every thought, word and action.

On one occasion my yogi friend explained how they meditate. 'We first of all sit comfortably. We are not concerned with particular postures. Nor do we concentrate on our breathing. Those are aspects of Hatha Yoga. In Raja Yoga we are only concerned with being soul-conscious and having divine union. We meditate with our eyes open because it is better for concentration and because we are learning to stay open-eyed in remembrance throughout the day. Our sitting meditation of the morning leads into our "walking-talking" meditation of the day. In effect yoga is our way of life, not just what happens when we meditate. We try to maintain our connection with God constantly. To whatever extent we achieve this, to that same extent we are sustained, cleansed and purified.'

'What, exactly, do you do when you meditate or have yoga?' I asked.

'Well, once comfortably seated, with the eyes open, we first explore our thoughts. We check the mind, and gently make it stable. We withdraw our thoughts from the body, the bodily relationships, the world around us, and from our roles and responsibilities. While doing this we apply a full stop to any wasteful or negative thoughts towards others. Before long we have the single awareness of being a soul, a point of light situated behind the centre of the forehead. Once stable like this, we next "fly" in the vehicle of the mind beyond this corporeal (physical) world, into a relationship with God.'

'You leave the body? I mean, does the soul leave the body in meditation?'

She smiled patiently. 'No. It is the mind that travels beyond the physical body and the material universe. It is the mind that experiences union or yoga with the Supreme. The mind is a faculty of the soul and it flies on the wings of thought, or on the wings of a pure desire. We call this the flying stage.'

'So,' I asked. 'Where do you fly to?'

'We remember our home in this stage, where we come from; the soul world or Nirvana. It is the "land" of peace, in a dimension beyond the physical universe. We remember God, the resident of this "land", as a most subtle point of loving energy. In this we experience our highest stage of pure silence. And it is here that we experience being in world service,' she paused briefly then continued. 'The other "destination" of the flying stage, is what we call the subtle region, a dimension God has created, between the incorporeal home and the corporeal world. It is a dimension of light and silence, created through purity.'

As she spoke, she seemed to pause between sentences in a hypnotic way that made one peaceful and attentive. 'We call this the realm of angels,' she said. 'It is an in-between place where we rediscover our own angelic qualities. In the subtle region, rather than as a point form, we experience ourselves as subtle light forms, whilst feeling free and bodiless.'

'Morning meditation establishes divine union with God every day.'

'And how do you end meditation?' I asked.

'We return to the awareness of our bodies, seated again in the centre of the forehead. But as we do so we maintain a "bodiless stage".'

'How do you mean, a bodiless stage?' I asked.

'By holding onto the experience of our form of light' she replied, 'we maintain our feelings of remembrance and divine union after returning to the physical. In remembrance throughout the day, we endeavour to retain the awareness of this subtle form whilst going about our business.'

'Is that where the traffic control fits in?' I asked, remembering our previous conversation.

'Yes,' she replied. 'Morning meditation establishes divine union with God every day. At traffic control, we keep refreshing the meditation experience. Effectively we remain meditative and in remembrance all the time. Yet to see us we are just ordinary, going about our business.'

From my experiences with the yogis of Mt Abu, I appreciated the constant attention and effort required to maintain union with the divine. Extrapolating to spiritual growth in general, we need to develop the habit of initially attaining union in morning meditation or prayer. Then, throughout the day, we need to maintain this connection through a practice of remembrance. At first this takes effort and self-discipline but soon becomes natural or 'second nature'.

TWENTY

Meditation Exercise: Divine Union and Remembrance

*T*his exercise represents the single most significant and influential method for self-realisation. On rising in the morning, make your first waking thought one of divinity, such as, 'I am a child of God,' or, 'I am one with the Universe.' Use whatever it is that makes you feel that you are in a divine relationship. It helps greatly if you spend ten or fifteen minutes before bedtime preparing your mind for these waking thoughts. Remember the mind 'travels' on the direction of its thoughts.

Next refresh yourself if necessary with a shower, tea or coffee. Do whatever it is that suits your preparation for the most valuable time you will spend each day. Then sit for meditation or prayer. Do so in a fixed place each day. By conducting a regular spiritual practice in the same location, you will create a conducive atmosphere for yourself and others.

Enter meditation as you have previously, though try to do so with your eyes open. This habit will better prepare you to maintain the experience throughout the day. During traffic control through the day it can be a little difficult to close your eyes without people noticing! When I was changing from closed to open-eyed meditation, I would begin with the eyes closed, then open them slowly once I was peaceful and relaxed. I would imagine that I was sitting behind the 'windows' of my eyes, just observing the field of vision, without attaching my attention to anything in it. Whilst doing so, I would keep my thoughts on the divine focus of meditation.

Another useful tip is to use a candle in a darkened room. Resting your eyes on the flame, use this as a focal point to develop *concentration*. After a while you will find yourself simply observing the flame, not concentrating on it. The candle flame could also represent the soul as a point of light energy.

Whether or not you find open-eyed meditation suitable, remove your thoughts from all attractions of the body, the world and relationships. Become aware of yourself in the form of spiritual light and connect yourself, through this awareness to your source of divinity. Use mental imagery, if you like, to invoke spiritual feelings. This can be either literal, such as imagining yourself walking through a forest, or abstract, such as visualising yourself in the company of angels. Alternatively you could read from an inspirational text before meditating.

As spiritual feelings enter your meditation, let yourself become silently surrendered and receive the company of the divine.

As spiritual feelings enter your meditation, let yourself become silently surrendered and *receive* the company of the divine. This is union. Hold on to it, experience it, value it, nurture it and *remember* it.

Stay like this for ten or fifteen minutes; the longer the better. Almost nobody can stop their mind having thoughts that interrupt such union. If the mind wanders, gently guide it back and re-establish the thoughts that created union. Alternatively you can simply observe distracting thoughts and let them pass by as if projected on a 'screen' in your mind. Experiment for yourself and see what works for you. Sometimes, when there are difficulties, it pays to stop for a few minutes, and start again.

Don't get frustrated or feel like you're failing. It defeats the purpose. I would say that 95% of my meditating life has been uneventful in terms of amazing experiences, yet eventful in terms of accelerated maturation. There were periods when I experienced nothing then, *in retrospect*, realised the benefit. We live in a 'quick fix' society today, where people are all too quick to say something doesn't work for them. Meditation or prayer requires patience, gentleness and ... *faith*. They are definitely beneficial.

When you complete your morning meditation, hold onto the experience of divine union as you re-enter the awareness of your body. Have a determined thought to stay in the company of the divine throughout the day. You could do so by being soul-conscious about yourself and others, or by considering the divine to be your friend and companion. Also have several periods of traffic control through the day. You will be amazed at how long two or three minutes seem when you stop. Yet this much time is easy to afford.

TWENTY-ONE

Attainments from the Path of Realisation

A t the end of 1998 I revisited the Brahma Kumaris in Mt Abu. During my stay I was asked to meet a group of Indian Raja Yoga students from Mysore, which has around five thousand developing yogis. Their regional coordinator was a serene image of purity and realisation.

Whenever she interacted, she became light, easy and happy, making others feel the same way. Immediately an interaction finished she withdrew into herself and became peaceful, creating an atmosphere around her of peace and power. She seemed to move from one state to the other with exquisite simplicity. I took great pleasure in her company and admired her economy. Whether in thoughts, words or actions, nothing was being wasted. There was no 'small talk', no awkwardness and no barriers. In one moment she was making people happy, in the next she was making them peaceful.

If I caught her eye for a few moments, my mind would empty of thoughts and fill with love and satisfaction. I had the impression that she was so full and contented in herself that her soul had no desire other than simply to *be*. Without desire there was complete acceptance and surrender in her, which appeared to automatically benefit everyone.

The atmosphere around her was similar to that of acceptance in the dying. It was also subtly different. When someone dies in acceptance, it follows a struggle in which everything is stripped away. Soul-consciousness is attained but usually without self-knowledge. What I observed in the yogi was complete self-control. She was surrendered and serving through her mind, her attitude and her presence. Her purity emanated a power that influenced without effort. In my eyes she was an angel and a world-server. Her spiritual attainments of soul-consciousness had come from the path of realisation, rather than by the force of circumstance. As she is living rather than dying, her potential to influence is substantial.

Her purity emanated a power that inflenced without effort.

In this world some stand out on the basis of their attainments. An athlete is visible when he or she is achieving, yet the discipline, effort and sacrifice involved are hidden. It is the expression or performance that makes people stand out in relation to their aims and objectives. Likewise, on the spiritual path it is attainment that makes a soul stand out.

We have already looked at the efforts, discipline and sacrifices required for successful meditation and self-transformation. To the best of my ability, I will now outline the attainments we can aim for on the path of realisation. Each of these can also be thought of as pure states of acceptance.

TWENTY-TWO

State of Attainment: Grace or Self - Sovereignty

*J*n Chapter 11, we encountered Margo's realisation that the beauty she sought externally, actually came from within. She was very much at peace when she died after my last visit to her home. Several months later I met her daughter Genaro, who spoke of their special time at the end. 'In the last week she stopped fighting and accepted everything. Everything about her had changed. It was like she just let go of all her fear and surrendered to God. I know it sounds crazy but being with her then was like being in the presence of God himself.'

'Yes, I felt that too,' I replied. 'I could see the change in her. All the suffering and struggle were finished. She was just being herself.'

'It was more than that,' Genaro continued. 'I really meant it was like being with God. It didn't seem like Mum at all. The only word that fits for me is grace. I read somewhere that grace is experienced when the nature of God manifests itself, here on earth. There was nothing in her heart but love, peace and happiness. When she looked at me I felt a current of love that made me forget everything.'

As she spoke I saw tears in her eyes. Not tears of sorrow but tears of beauty and wonder. 'At first I really missed her but she appeared to me one night, a few weeks after leaving her body. She didn't say a word. She just stood at the end of my bed dressed as a North American Indian, looking young and vital, and surrounded in light. She looked at me in the same way as before, removing all my sorrow with the love and grace of her presence. After she left I spent all night feeling warm and happy. I had the thought that I was to tell you of this encounter. I think it is something you are meant to learn.'

Touched by this I said, 'Thank you. It is about grace, I'm sure of it. It has been on my mind for the last week. It's amazing that you should choose this moment. If you'd come to me when this happened it wouldn't have meant so much. Serendipity really does come into our lives when we walk the spiritual path.'

Looking at Genaro I asked, 'Have you seen her since then.' Smiling, Genaro replied, 'No, but I often feel her presence. I don't think I will see her again. I don't feel I need to. I know she is alive and well, a living angel with the grace of God. What more can I ask for?'

'Only one thing,' I replied. 'To become like her yourself.'

Genaro looked at me first with surprise then with understanding. 'So she has brought us together to teach me something also. For you it is about grace. For me it is to recognise in her, my own potential.' This struck a chord in me. 'Yes, and I've just realised something else,' I said. 'Through her grace you had thought of her as special. Instead you were meant to recognise your own potential.' There is something here for us all to understand. To think of someone as special is to separate ourselves from our own potential. We should appreciate the beauty of others and live up to it in ourselves.

'So wherever we find grace,' Genaro continued, 'its real purpose is to show us who we truly are. It's an expression not only of God but also of our own potential. It's as if

God is trying to show us that we can be like Him.'

The *Oxford Dictionary* defines grace as 'the unmerited favour of God', reflecting a Christian perspective that we are unworthy. But why would God give grace to the unworthy? To me this seems senseless. Yet it would seem equally profane for others to entertain grace as a human potential. They think that it can only come from God. I believe this to be a conditioned attitude of body-consciousness. Margo's example shows us that grace is also plausible in human terms.

When acceptance develops in the terminally ill, it generally does so after yielding to loss. When soul-consciousness develops through spiritual effort, its basis is faith and self-realisation. Grace emerges in the personality, attitude, words or actions under either circumstance. Whether its attainment follows suffering or enlightened effort-making, grace can hardly be considered an 'unmerited favour of God'. Its human potential has something to do with the inner-self.

Nevertheless grace remains ill-defined. Where does it come from, and how does spiritual endeavour lead to grace? How can a human being be like God? What are the characteristics that enable a human to *be* grace? When I was originally in Mt Abu I asked these questions of my adopted yogi friend and concluded, 'How do we conduct ourselves with grace?'

'Here we talk about *self-sovereignty*,' she replied. 'When grace is to be found in a human being, there will be sovereignty over the senses. Normally our senses have control over us, making us act and react in certain ways. If we see something happen, or hear about something, we easily become angry, sad or excited. We soon start thinking and speaking of what we saw or heard, creating negative or "wasteful" vibrations through our thoughts, words and actions. Such influences make the state of grace elusive.'

I interjected, 'Hear no evil, see no evil, and speak no evil.'

She smiled generously, 'Yes, the three wise monkeys is a good tale and relevant to what I was saying.' She thought for a moment. 'But when we think of evil here, we really mean the vices of body-consciousness. The five "evil spirits" are anger, lust, attachment, ego and greed. In body-consciousness, ego takes the support of these vices through the senses. Desire "pulls" us towards sense-gratification and the soul becomes dependent. When we renounce these dependencies and surrender to God, the senses no longer "pull" us in other directions. The challenge is for us to take control of the senses and to use them for divine service.'

I considered this for a moment and asked, 'So do you just ignore what is happening in the world?'

'Not ignore,' she replied. 'But we detach through knowledge, understanding and faith. We have faith that all is in divine order and that God is now revealing Himself to transform the world. With this knowledge we do not concern ourselves with the problems around us. Instead we accept everything with the understanding that God has the power to change everything. By staying in yoga (meditative union with God) at all times we fulfil our role of being co-operative with the Supreme. In this hidden and unheralded way, we are helping in God's task of solving the problems of the world.'

I sought further clarification, 'You mentioned seeing, hearing and speaking. How about the other senses and what exactly is self-sovereignty?'

'We free ourselves from the desire to touch and the need for physical expressions of intimacy,' she replied. 'We have love for one-another but it is expressed spiritually through cooperation and eye contact. We eat for the livelihood of our body. We enjoy the food but have no greed or attachment to it. We are not repelled by anything, as this is also body-consciousness. Whether it relates to particular smells, behaviour or personalities, nothing repels a graceful nature. Grace is like a rose, which remains constantly open, fragrant and beautiful for all to appreciate. It does not withdraw fragrance or colour from someone with a bad nature, and it is up to us whether or not we appreciate it.'

'So grace or self-sovereignty means to have complete control over the senses,' I said.

'Yes, this is the aim,' she continued. 'If you like, think of the body as your kingdom and your "self" as the ruler or the sovereign. The senses are your ministers. They should work for you and you should serve through them. They should be cooperative with your directions ...'

'But they run amok half of the time,' I interrupted. 'They are forever chasing after one thing or another. If it's not relationships, it's possessions or the desire to see this, experience that and taste the other!'

'Yes,' she laughed. 'This is what happens in body-consciousness. The ministers of the kingdom run amok. Instead of ruling over your senses, you become subservient as they rule over you. In this world today everyone has forgotten who they are, and everyone is ruled by the desire for "sense gratification". Under such circumstances no one can experience or express grace.

'... think of the body as your kingdom and your "self" as the ruler or the sovereign.'

'Through yoga we enter into a relationship with God, that enables us to progressively "cool" down the senses. Eventually we can relate through them, without being "pulled" by them. When all our satisfaction comes from the divine, we have no dependencies of body-consciousness and therefore no other desires. When there are no desires left for the self, then we are soul-conscious ...'

'And full of grace,' I added.

'With self-sovereignty,' she said, 'instead of being influenced by things we see, hear or feel, we learn to appreciate the divinity in everyone. With self-sovereignty, our senses communicate respect and good wishes for all.'

My next statement also expressed my experience of her company. 'And when people come into connection with grace and self-sovereignty, they are inspired to change themselves.'

'Yes,' she continued. 'Which is the most honest form of service in the world today. As *we* attain sovereignty over the senses, *they* in turn cooperate with the divine, to bring peace and harmony into the world. The senses become instruments of the soul. And the soul, in turn, becomes an instrument of God.

'When we have surrendered completely and the instrument is clear, egoless and free from desire, the flow of grace from the divine is unobstructed.'

Thus the state of grace or self-sovereignty is one of surrender and self-control. Now free from desire, the soul has nothing to lose and nothing to fear. All that remains is love. This is grace.

TWENTY-THREE

State of Attainment: The Karmateet Stage

K armateet is a Hindi (Indian) word, which means
'karma-free'. The word karma, literally translated,
means 'action'. Karma-free means that the soul is
no longer burdened by the sanskaras of its past negative
actions. These have been settled such that there is no influence of fear or guilt on how we behave. In a sense the soul
has been forgiven for, or cleansed of, its past actions. The
resulting karmateet stage is one of love, benevolence and
service, where every thought and action brings benefit to
the world. To grasp this notion we need to first understand
the law of karma.

As the law of karma is generally considered an Eastern
philosophy, it is often forgotten that it is reflected in
Christian teachings. In his letter to the Gelatians, Paul
wrote: 'For whatsoever a man soeth, that shall he also reap'
(Gelatians 6:7). The basic premise here is that we will
receive the return of our actions and experience life
accordingly. Right action is rewarded with good fortune,
whilst suffering is the consequence of wrong actions from
the past.

The contentious issue is around the question of rebirth,
which is contrary to orthodox Christian teaching. Years
ago, in my early days of meditation, I followed a self-training

manual called *A Course in Miracles* (Foundation of Inner Peace, Viking Penguin, New York, 1996). This holds that the concept of rebirth is immaterial, as the soul has only one spiritual life. Whether or not the soul adopts different physical forms is of no consequence, as there remains but the one life. *A Course in Miracles* holds that the real spiritual challenge is to develop a divine perception of the world around us, to let go of fear and to return to love.

In Chapter 11 we met Margo in a state of acceptance before she died. When I originally met her she was utterly shocked, angry and confused by her diagnosis of cancer. 'Why me?' she lamented. 'What have I done to deserve this? I've lead a good life and taken care of myself. I don't smoke or drink and I care about others. The world is full of bad people who abuse themselves and others. How could God do this to me and let them get off "scot-free"? It's just not fair!'

As we have seen, Margo moved on from here but this question of shock and disbelief is very common. Where did the disease come from? Why has it happened? Why now? I sometimes encounter the more complex issue of someone associating his or her situation with a specific past action.

Manifred was admitted to our palliative care unit with metastatic pancreas cancer. He was in a very terminal state, extremely wasted, dependent and suffering from chronic severe pain. The pain was unusual, however, in that it was non-specific and generalised. It didn't accord with the distribution of the cancer and didn't respond to pain killers. He seemed tormented and I wondered if his pain was related to some form of spiritual despair.

When I explored this, he told me that he was sure he was being punished. During the Second World War he had a role in which he had to torture prisoners, sometimes to death. Very distraught, he told me with explicit detail some of the more sickening instances. For nearly half an hour he confessed all, then said he was certain that his past actions were related to him getting cancer. Once the guilt had been expressed, his torment subsided and the pain became manageable. He died within forty-eight hours but needed to be sedated towards the end to relieve his restlessness.

Whether Manifred's suffering was attributed to his wartime activities I cannot say. I do believe, however, that the soul is accountable for its actions. While Manifred was clearly tormented by guilt, I also feel his intuition reflected a hidden awareness of karmic laws. Actions leave sanskaras (subconscious impressions) on the soul. Good actions accumulate benefit for the soul and are returned as good fortune. Such fortune might be realised immediately, as in a reward for generosity, or it might be kept 'in stock' for a future life or 'birth'. Charity in one life, for instance, could lead to wealth in the next. Negative actions that are selfish or cause sorrow also have their karmic returns. These will manifest as some form of suffering which can also be immediate or delayed. If the return is delayed, then that account is kept 'in stock' within the sanskaras for settlement in a future birth.

It is somewhat like having a karmic 'bank account' within the soul, which is debited by bad actions and credited by good ones. Before coming into physical form, the soul had a clean slate with neither positive nor negative accounts. As I discussed earlier, the soul is deceived by body-consciousness and progressively loses its innocence. As its purity reduces, its accounts accumulate a progressive karmic debt. From time to time the soul's accounts have to be balanced, its sanskaras cleared and its original karmateet (karma-free) stage re-established.

Many souls are born with the primary purpose of clearing their karmic accounts. Consequently there are many dying whilst still young. I always look on a child with cancer as an old soul. Having remained innocent from birth, a cancer develops despite the absence of significant karmic accounts from this lifetime. I remember one child called Jordan because his mother, Lucy, was quite remarkable. She thought of Jordan as a wise old soul who had been sent to teach her.

At two years of age, Jordan developed a neuroblastoma in his pelvis, which had already spread to the liver and bone-marrow. Neuroblastoma is the fourth commonest child-hood malignancy and affects about ten out of every million children. When it presents in infants less than one year-old, it is generally curable. When it develops in older children, and has already spread at the time of diagnosis, cure is usually elusive. It is a frustrating disease for those who treat cancer because it usually presents with extensive secon-daries in the older children. Although it responds well to chemotherapy initially, it generally recurs and becomes resistant to treatment.

The cancer specialist told Lucy all of this and summed up, 'About seventy per cent of children respond to chemo-therapy and one in five can live for more than three years. Without treatment Jordan will die within a few months.' She decided to go ahead with chemotherapy, which was the only option really.

Lucy told me that the treatment was a nightmare. Over the next six months Jordan went for regular chemo-therapy. The treatment was aggressive; it made him very sick and all the hair on his body fell out, even his eye-brows. He required two additional hospital admissions for serious infections brought on by the chemotherapy. Lucy said the whole thing was nearly unbearable for her and that Jordan was terrified every time he went to hospital. Nevertheless it worked and Jordan's cancer went into com-plete remission.

Lucy was overjoyed and naturally hopeful that he was cured. From that point on, Jordan had to see doctors regularly and was admitted to have scans and other tests every three months. His growth was stunted and normal development was delayed. Otherwise all went well for nearly three years. Then Lucy was given the terrible news that the cancer had returned and more chemotherapy was needed to keep Jordan alive. 'It won't cure him though,' she was told.

It all started again. The disease in Jordan's body was partially controlled this time. He hated hospitals and doctors, and created a fuss every time his therapy was due. After two months Lucy refused to let them treat him any further but she agreed to continue with regular check-ups. As Jordan's condition deteriorated she was put under pressure for him to go back on chemotherapy, and was made to feel responsible for him getting worse. Jordan's stomach swelled up with the disease and his ribs fractured. He was put on morphine for pain control, he became constipated and vomited frequently.

Lucy refused to see the specialist any more. Concerned about Jordan's welfare the paediatrician contacted me and asked if I could get involved as a palliative care doctor. He expressed particular concern for the child. He believed that Lucy had distanced herself emotionally to the point that she was neglecting Jordan. In fact the specialist was quite angry. 'I think she is irresponsible,' he told me. 'She doesn't seem to care about Jordan. She seems distant and quite detached from how seriously ill he is. We feel she may be neglecting the child's emotional needs and are concerned about her lack of intimacy.'

I contacted Lucy and she agreed for me to visit Jordan, who was now five years-old. I wasn't sure what to expect or whether I would be able to help. I was particularly concerned about the question of abuse as I had no experience in this. As it turned out, I was pleasantly surprised. There was clearly a close love bond between them and Lucy seemed committed to Jordan's welfare. Jordan was very unwell with a huge abdomen, sunken eyes and a frightened face. Lucy smiled apologetically, 'I'm afraid he's seen too many doctors. He's afraid of the things you do to him; and afraid that you might put him in hospital.'

Returning her smile I said, 'Don't worry, I'll work things out with you. You know Jordan better than anyone so we'll see what the problems are first. I'll have a talk to him before I go and only examine him if it is absolutely necessary.' Lucy looked relieved and put on a video for Jordan to watch. He brightened up immediately, realising that I wasn't about to do anything nasty to him.

Lucy and I discussed their experiences in the next room. She was grateful for the opportunity to talk, especially when I agreed that refusing chemotherapy was in Jordan's best interests. By that stage it couldn't cure him and was causing more suffering than his disease. At the end I asked Lucy how she felt about Jordan, his illness and the fact that she would lose him soon.

At twenty-four years, Lucy replied with a depth that astounded me. 'I'm not worried about him,' she replied. 'I know he is a wise old soul who has come here to settle his accounts and to teach me. I also believe that he will be going on from here to become a great soul. I don't feel I will lose him and I think of us as eternally bound. I only hope it won't take too long and that he won't have to suffer too much.'

'You believe in reincarnation, then,' I said.

'Yes,' she continued. 'And I've read a great deal about it in the last three years. Only special souls get sick and die when they are as young as Jordan. They really come to teach us and move on. Having Jordan is the greatest gift I have ever received. A clairvoyant told me at the beginning that he would only be here for a short time. She said I needed to exchange my love for his greater wisdom.'

'Does Jordan know this?' I asked.

She laughed. 'No. I've tried to talk to him about it but he doesn't understand. He's seen other kids with cancer and knows one or two who have died. He believes in life after death and still talks to them sometimes, as if they were in the room with him.' She thought for a moment, then continued. 'He once told me that we go up to heaven when we die, then, when it's our turn, God sends us down to a new life. Where he got that from, I'll never know. My clairvoyant told me that young children still remember where they've come from for a while. She also said that we forget our purpose for coming here, and that Jordan would not understand his spiritual evolution until he leaves his body.'

We talked for some time about spirituality and our reason for being. We had much in common in our philosophy and outlook, so I was quite free to express my beliefs without being intrusive. I assured her that we would not make Jordan go to hospital, and that we would do everything to make his death at home comfortable. Over the next few days we were successful in controlling the pain, constipation and vomiting. Consequently, over the last six weeks of his life Jordan was comfortable and relatively happy. I became his favourite doctor because I left him alone! Towards the end he went into a coma due to kidney failure and died very peacefully.

One other interesting thing happened. After my first interview with Lucy, I rang the paediatrician to reassure him of Jordan's welfare. I told him about Lucy's way of seeing things and that I felt she was close and loving towards the child. Her apparent distancing, I thought, reflected her spiritual awareness. This included her acceptance of Jordan's death. I said that I thought she was a good mother and I didn't think that Jordan was being neglected.

In response the paediatrician was angry. He clearly thought that I was an eccentric and that Jordan now needed his supervision. He said it was imperative that he see Jordan on a regular basis. I contacted Lucy diplomatically and told her that the specialist would still like to see Jordan. But the relationship had broken down long before — perhaps when she felt forced to accept further chemotherapy — and Lucy did not go back with Jordan.

In regard to the law of karma, I believe that Jordan was clearing past accounts in this birth. A disease of such complexity can only emerge in an experienced soul. When a new soul takes its first birth, its slate is clean with no sanskaras capable of manifesting disease in childhood. To develop childhood cancer, to be born with a deformity, or to be 'developmentally delayed' all require the experience and accounts of past births; so these are always old souls. Observing children with cancer is one of the influences that has convinced me of past lives.

When I was involved with Jordan, Lucy asked a question I hear frequently, 'Dr Cole, how can you do this sort of work? Don't you find it sad and depressing? It must be hard for you, knowing that you can't change anything.' It is a question I have given a considerable amount of thought to. My reply began like this, 'With people like yourself and Jordan there is a sense that nothing more can be done. In fact you often feel deserted when medical treatment has failed. Our approach in palliative care is much different. We understand that much can be done to control pain and suffering. We also understand how much it means to have support at times like this. We love to see the difference this makes, so our work is very rewarding.'

The second part of my reply had to do with spirituality. 'The other thing that keeps me happy in this work is my outlook on life. I have recognised my own eternal identity, so I see this in others also. No one dies and suffering is but a temporary period of adjustment for the soul. I don't really witness the suffering, I observe it and offer comfort. What

I see is a soul beginning to realise its full potential through clearing the karmic accounts of past births. In this way I can remain detached from the suffering, yet be close and loving in the relationship. Instead of worrying about my patients I send them love. I figure that love has more value than worry.'

I don't see suffering as a 'just desert' or look on it as a form of punishment. I see it as a natural process, which cleanses and purifies the soul. I think of it as concealed growth in which past karma is being settled at a personal level through illness. The soul is being set free and benefit will ultimately come. This may happen in the absence of spiritual awareness, yet it is a spiritual process.

According to the law of karma there are no accidents, coincidences or luck.

Apart from the karma of illnesses, we may also develop specific group or relationship karma. As a consequence of the past we find ourselves in relationships with people we have accounts with. We have no knowledge of our past-life encounters and find ourselves settling accounts by serving those souls, suffering in a relationship or causing someone pain.

Group settlement might take the form of an accident or a calamity, such as a plane crash or an earthquake. According to the law of karma there are no accidents, coincidences or luck. Whatever happens in life has been determined by past actions and relationships have already been established.

It is not essential that a soul suffers to settle its past accounts, though this can't always be avoided. When the soul is enlightened it engages the path of realisation and its growth is revealed. Within suffering, spiritual growth is concealed; whereas within enlightenment, it is apparent to the self and others. When we come into a relationship with the divine we can directly clear our accounts and old sanskaras. We also learn how to serve humanity through our nature and attitudes. On the basis of human service, spiritual relationship and divine union we can also move along to our karmateet stage. To whatever extent we succeed in these three, to that extent we limit our potential for suffering.

Once karmateet, the soul sees the world with deep love, understanding and detachment. It is then a divine image, beyond fear, doubt or desire. The karmateet stage is the end of our cycle from purity, through body-consciousness and back to purity. At the outset we are innocent yet vulnerable to a world we haven't experienced. At the end we are innocent yet knowledgeable of a world we understand.

TWENTY-FOUR

State of Attainment: Complete with All Powers

As we become soul-conscious we progressively develop self-respect based on spiritual awareness. This enables us to see the world differently, through a divine vision of brotherhood. In the East, such spiritual awakening and perceptual clarity is referred to as the 'third eye' opening. When conditioned by body-consciousness, the spiritual knowledge, virtues and powers of the soul become latent. Though present, they are hidden and obscured from expression. When we meditate and make spiritual effort, we gradually draw on this latency and these qualities resurface.

Raja Yoga meditation teaches that soul-consciousness is attained through self-knowledge, divine union, pure expression and human service. Once complete with all powers, knowledge and virtues, the soul is said to be in its highest stage. We have already entertained knowledge of our eternal identity throughout this book. We have also seen how to develop our virtues, and how to discern these in others. We will now consider how to awaken and utilise eight specific powers of the mind.

In the first instance we apply these to break the habits and conditioning of body-consciousness. Later, when we have become soul-conscious, they simply form part of a loving and virtuous nature. I will first outline the application of spiritual powers to growth and transformation, then describe their natural expression when we are soul-conscious.

The *eight powers* enable us to control and focus the flow of our thoughts and actions. Through clarity, consistency and integrity, they make us trustworthy and influential without being forceful or controlling. They give us the ability to recognise truth, to succeed in our spiritual objectives and to uphold our spiritual identity in a body-conscious world.

The ***power to withdraw*** enables us to become introverted where situations might otherwise have influenced or affected us. This power was part of the yogi's 'economy' described in Chapter 21. Withdrawing into herself she could disengage, centre herself in truth and make the atmosphere peaceful. It is particularly important to practise withdrawing, so it is easy to achieve when there is disturbance around you. When someone starts to gossip, criticise or get angry, withdraw into your awareness of being a soul. Instead of becoming involved in something wasteful, become introverted and simply observe it like a scene in a drama. This habit makes you less vulnerable and preserves your peace of mind. You also reduce the risk of spreading someone else's negativity.

The ***power to pack-up*** means to apply a full stop in the mind. Instead of thinking or worrying about people or situations, we develop the power to complete a task or interaction and then pack-up our thoughts. Once it has past, we don't waste our energy wondering about the consequences. This enables us to always give our full attention and energy to the present moment. By stopping us from worrying about problems, the power to pack-up is a form of mind control that prevents negative expansion from occurring.

Such expansion can make little problems seem big, leading to complexity, anxiety and stress. When we apply a full stop, even a big problem is seen more clearly and becomes small.

The *power to face* means to have courage and a capacity to change. Whilst cultivating our inner beauty we must also recognise, acknowledge and free ourselves from weaknesses. Just as we need courage to face the challenges of our external world, we need courage to face weaknesses inherent to our body-conscious nature and conditioning. When we are challenged or criticised this is an opportunity to see our weaknesses, if we have enough self-respect and honesty. Don't be hurt but look to see if there is the slightest justification.

- Has someone seen something that I can change?
- Was I a little forceful?
- Did I really give my full attention to their position?
- Is there still some arrogance within me?
- Was I lacking in tolerance?

After checking yourself you can resolve to change some aspect. In this way those who become 'obstacles' in our lives actually challenge us to become stronger and grow spiritually.

With the *power to tolerate* we maintain equanimity, whilst constantly giving regard to others. This enables us to remain easy and make others relaxed. True tolerance does not mean to tolerate someone with feelings of dislike and tension. It is a feeling of love and understanding, in which we maintain good wishes even for those who try to hurt or defame us. We can understand why people misbehave when we realise that wrong action comes from body-consciousness. When you tolerate in this way there is an automatic feeling of forgiveness. You don't even begin to be judgemental, so remain unaffected by wrong attitudes, words and actions. True tolerance is a disposition of love towards a world of conflict and illusion.

The *power to accommodate* means to make room in the heart for everyone. Whether or not we agree, there is respect for different views or opinions and only love is returned to those with a negative or irritating disposition. As an ocean merges a raindrop, so too accommodation power enables us to merge difficult situations and conflicts within the self. When something unexpected happens you remain unaffected, as the power to accommodate fortifies your capacity to love.

The *power to discriminate* is a discerning intellect, which recognises spiritual values and acts accordingly. The more we pay attention to this, the more accurate we become. When giving, distinguish which thoughts, words or actions will impart peace or happiness, and elect never to cause sorrow. When receiving, take nothing from others that would cause unhappiness or make you body-conscious. If someone offered you a piece of rotting fruit, you wouldn't take it except to be polite and accommodating. You certainly wouldn't eat it. So if someone speaks to you with anger, jealousy or greed, listen if you must but don't digest what is said or take it away with you. If someone tries to influence you with dishonesty, turn away. If someone tries to spoil your view of another person, do not enter into it. Look for and accept only virtues from others. In the spiritual effort of appreciation (Chapter 11), we determined to always look beyond weaknesses and seek qualities within others. This was about using the power of discrimination to receive spiritually. You attain this power when you can distinguish virtues and leave 'rubbish' behind.

The *power of judgement* makes us accurate in decision-making and action. Clearly this requires a discerning intellect and the power of discrimination. Once you have discerned with spiritual accuracy you then use judgement about your action. It is possible to discriminate effectively, yet misjudge the reactions of others. You may act with the best of intentions, yet offend or impose on someone. Don't think they lack gratitude but face the fact that your judgement may have been weak. To develop the power of judgement, check the results of words or actions against the question, 'Was there benefit, or did someone suffer?' And that question should include you.

With the *power to cooperate* we make the task of world benefit easy. We use this power to spread spiritual feelings and values, which is a means of cooperating with the divine. When you give trust to others you increase their self-confidence, and when you communicate your motives you make them feel part of a whole. *When you give trust to others you increase their self-confidence, and when you communicate your motives you make them feel part of a whole.* When you give cooperation in this way, you will receive it from everyone. Your power of cooperation thereby influences the spread of spiritual attitudes.

So the eight spiritual powers taught in Raja Yoga are to withdraw, to pack-up, to face, to tolerate, to accommodate, to discriminate, to judge and to cooperate. When they are working in unison with spiritual knowledge and virtues, the soul becomes complete and attains purity. Such a soul is stable, mature and gentle. It is compassionate and giving, and remains constantly at peace with itself. Unattached, yet responsive and loving, it combines the perfect balance of firmness and flexibility whilst *accommodating* any situation with love. Centred in truth, a pure soul exercises wisdom, courage and cleanliness as it *withdraws* from any disturbance of waste or negativity. It is understanding and benevolent, whilst treating everyone with respect and humility. Such a soul remains unaffected as it deals with problems then *packs-up*. By never going into expansion the soul remains light and contented, warm and accessible. It is fearless, with the power *to face* any of life's challenges. This soul recognises its own value and *cooperates* with the service of human enlightenment. Whilst cooperating it *discriminates* accurately, and only gives cooperation to that which brings benefit. Surrendered and free, a pure soul has clear *judgement*, and expresses natural authority with no need for force. Obedient to the directions of the divine, such a soul is rich and forgiving in its capacity to *tolerate*.

Surrendered and free, a pure soul has clear judgement, and expresses natural authority with no need for force.

On the path of realisation we ultimately attain all powers and become free from body-consciousness. With meditation we identify the eight powers then use them to break body-consciousness, and to serve others. As soul-consciousness emerges, we express the powers effortlessly with only our virtues visible. With this effort, in time, the soul returns to love and is an image of love.

TWENTY-FIVE

State of Attainment: A World Server

*A*ll spiritual and religious teachings include human service as an essential component of expression and development. Spiritual growth along the path of realisation is no exception. We can serve through what *we do* for others and through who we are. During my life as a palliative care physician I have come to realise that *what we do* is a limited form of service. It is the service of *who we are*, which can be truly far-reaching. If we are soul-conscious whilst serving others then the quality of our attention or care is greatly enhanced. If through remembrance we sustain ourselves when not involved with others, then we emanate peace through this expression of faith. If we are contented whilst conducting mundane tasks then we influence those who witness our happiness. These are aspects of natural, effortless service that comes from one's attitude and perspective.

In Chapter 4, I discussed my encounter with latent spiritual possibilities following a post-cathartic experience of love. Encounters like this are 'spiritual windows' that offer a glimpse of our full potential and bring new insights and enthusiasm for the journey. My second 'window' experience occurred in 1992, on a mountain summit in India during a sunrise meditation. I had an experience of unity, in which all boundaries between myself and others became artificial. There was very little sense of my own identity. It seemed as if I had dissolved and become part of all that *is*. At the same time I felt at one with God. It was as if my soul, the divine and everything else were in union. For twenty minutes, as pink pastels succumbed to a blue sky, I feel that I became an instrument of love. Through meditation I had stepped out of the way and allowed God to reach my soul and work through me.

I discovered later that this was what they describe in Raja Yoga as the 'seed' stage of meditation. It is a state of divine union in which one becomes 'bodiless', and an instrument for world service. With magical simplicity the soul becomes a pure, unobstructed channel for spiritual love, which seeks out the sensitive, awakens the ready and enlightens the worthy. Such world service is both unique and unlimited. Unique because it extends directly from the divine, through an individual to the world. Unlimited because there is no need for proximity or contact. World service contrasts with the limitations of more familiar worldly service, where we rush around in our work roles or engage in charitable work. Such service is limited by our body-consciousness. While compassionate support for one-another is essential, the service of divine union and surrender has a 'far-reaching' quality.

It was as if my soul, the divine and everything else were in union.

About a year after my trip to Mt Abu I received confirmation of this, following a similar meditation experience at my home. On that occasion I sat and developed the awareness of being a soul, a subtle point of divine light. From this point, in the centre of my forehead, I connected with the divine nature, personality and purity of God. As I felt the 'current' of this union, I again experienced the seed stage. I had a particular awareness of divine love passing through me to everyone I had been connected with, past and present. As I left the meditation I had the clear feeling that service had been done. I was also aware that we can settle our karmic accounts through meditation. These accounts keep us bound to relationships with certain souls who receive love and power through our meditation.

Later that same day, Fran came to my office saying that she needed to speak to me. I had known Fran for years as an oncology and palliative care nurse. She'd had some back problems and I had supported her application for a job that didn't require heavy lifting. Fran had a dream the night before and felt compelled to tell me about it. 'I was climbing a mountain without ropes or assistance. As I was nearing the top I became tired and reached an overhang. It was very dangerous but I had no choice but to proceed, as going back was impossible. Anyway, I started to climb the overhang but I was very tired and got stuck with a sheer drop below me. I was terrified. At that moment, just before I fell, you appeared beside me and helped me over the last part.'

Fran seemed slightly embarrassed as she looked at me. 'But it wasn't really to do with you. I woke up knowing that it was really to do with God. The dream reassured me that there is nothing to fear in the future. I know help will always be there whatever obstacles I face. It has given me confidence.'

I sat in wonder, feeling that she had been 'sent' to validate my meditation experience. I told her about my morning meditation and how I thought it was related to her dream and realisation. 'What time was it when you woke up?' I asked. 'Just before four-thirty,' she replied, which was during my meditation.

There are two things that especially touched me. The first was Fran's awareness that her support came from God, even though I was the figure in the dream. This fits well with the idea that we become instruments of the divine as we surrender and 'allow' God. Second, Fran hadn't been in my mind during meditation, yet had an experience through our connection. It taught me that if we remove the blocks from our minds, we can realise an unlimited potential to serve from afar. Once sceptical of the 'absent healing' conducted by some prayer and meditation groups, I now had to accept its validity.

It is possible to become a constant world server when we are experienced in meditation. With the capacity to withdraw at will, we can adopt the 'bodiless' seed-stage in a natural, easy way without appearing to meditate. Our original virtues and powers emerge and every thought carries purity and goodwill to the world. Absent healing is the very nature of one who has the spiritual attainment of a world server.

TWENTY-SIX

State of Attainment: The Stage of an Angel

Ralph was 'ordinary': a sixty-three year-old carpenter who had lung cancer. I met him ten days before his death, following his admission to the hospice. He was distressed with pain, breathless, and very frightened. He didn't really understand what was happening but knew that people with cancer died in our establishment. I spent some time with him, reviewing his recent history and checking his chest X-ray. Apart from being breathless, he didn't look too bad and I didn't think his death was imminent.

I told him this, 'Ralph, the cancer is quite advanced on your X-ray and it is making you short of breath. But, comparing it with an X-ray from two months ago, it hasn't been growing too fast. I just think that it's got to a stage where it's making you breathless. I really don't think you are dying at the present moment.' I noticed that he was calmer and was giving me his full attention. I could see he was eager to be informed and wanted to know why things were changing. I talked to him about cancer and showed him the X-rays to help him understand. 'What we need to do now is to control the pain and breathlessness with small doses of regular morphine. I think you will be much more comfortable by later this afternoon.'

We spoke for a while longer about the treatment. Towards the end I asked him, 'Is there anything that you're particularly afraid of at the moment?' He replied, 'Yes, I'm terrified that I will suffocate and choke to death.' This is an extremely common fear of anyone who has experienced breathlessness with lung cancer. I consoled him in this way, 'At the moment I believe you will improve. If, by any chance, things were to get worse then we would offer you sedation. We don't allow people to die struggling for breath here. We would keep you asleep so you wouldn't be aware of any feelings in your body.'

He looked relieved and squeezed my arm as I left. Now that he was informed, he felt reassured and trusting of his care-givers. When I returned a week later he was no longer breathless, was pain-free and was now quite calm. However, he was also much weaker and it was evident that he would die soon. We talked about the increasing weakness and I asked him how he felt about it. 'I don't think there's much hope, is there?' he replied. 'How do you mean: not much hope?' I asked, to which he said, 'Well, I'm not going to get better, am I?'

We went on to discuss his prognosis and the fact that he wouldn't live very much longer. He wasn't distressed at all by the frankness of our talk. In fact he was relieved to know what was going to happen and appreciated my openness. He said that living had become a struggle and he was happy that he didn't have to fight any more. On my final visit he looked peaceful and was sleeping. I wouldn't have disturbed him but he opened his eyes as I was turning to leave. Clear, blue and contented, they contrasted with the frightened, furtive eyes of just over a week ago.

Sitting up, he smiled at me as I asked him how he was feeling. The answer was quite surprising and disarming. 'I feel like I'm blessing everyone.' As he said this, I found myself experiencing a profound sense of peace in his presence. 'After you spoke to me that first time, I was so much easier on the inside,' he continued. 'I knew what was going on and why I was deteriorating. It took all my fear away. I was never frightened of dying, actually, but I was afraid of pain and suffering. You don't know what it meant to discover that I wouldn't choke to death.'

After a moment he said, 'On the second occasion you confirmed what I already knew — that I was dying. It felt wonderful afterwards and I just let go of everything. I stopped fighting and struggling. In fact I have been feeling better than I can ever remember. I've been completely at peace just lying here. I can hardly describe what it is like. I'm ready to die but in no hurry to do so. As long as I feel like this, I'm happy to be around.'

'Have a go at telling me what it feels like,' I suggested. 'As I said,' he continued thoughtfully, 'I feel like I'm blessing everyone. I'm incredibly light, almost floating. And it feels like I'm surrounded in light, as if there is a huge cocoon or halo all around me. At times I can even see it. I lie here feeling like I'm rising from my body and just keep observing light all around me. There are even moments when I feel that I'm a part of it.' While he was speaking, I found myself experi-encing the things he was describing and suddenly realised that he truly was blessing everyone. We seemed somehow connected and, when there was eye contact, it felt nothing like the company of a mortal being.

Ralph carried on, 'Although I'm lying here, I don't feel limited to my body. If I think of anyone, past or present, it feels like I'm instantly with that person and that my company is a blessing. Although I'm definitely in this body, it seems as if my mind can be extended beyond it. And it feels as if I'm travelling in the light that I was describing.' He paused, searching. 'There is one other thing that I can identify. There is nothing but love, inside and out. It seems that I have become love.'

Ralph was tired by the effort of talking and needed to rest again. As I left, I glanced back from the doorway. His eyes were half-open, gazing into the distance. He looked beautiful. I couldn't see the light that he had described but I could feel it. Ralph continued to deteriorate but he remained peaceful and didn't need the sedation we had discussed. He really did leave his body the next day and everyone remarked how they had felt blessed by him. On admission to the hospice, Ralph was an ordinary, frightened man with cancer. By the time he left he was almost an 'angel'.

I learnt something of the angelic stage of spiritual attainment from Ralph. He taught me that it is a state of mind. He also helped me to understand the subtle nature of the soul and its capacity to extend itself through the vehicle of the mind. When I was in Mt Abu, an experienced yogi described to me an ethereal realm she called the *subtle region*. She said it was an intermediate dimension of purity and light between the 'soul world' and the corporeal physical world. It is a 'place' where we are able to experience our subtle light-form, as well as our 'angelic' nature, which is pure, carefree and light in character. Ralph reflected this before leaving his body. He seemed to be free of his body and its limitations, whilst still in it.

As I left, I glanced back from the doorway. His eyes were half-open, gazing into the distance. He looked beautiful.

Meditation also teaches us to become 'bodiless' whilst still in the body. Bodiless here means to have no remaining trace of body-consciousness. As with Ralph and other examples of acceptance, the mind is no longer drawn to superficial concerns and is free from desire. When there is such purity, the mind can enter the subtle region at will. One may then reach others through thoughts, whilst experiencing the presence of light. It is generally more accurate to say that this 'light' is experienced rather than seen, although there are sensitive souls who seem able to witness it. Examples include those who can see auras and others with the psychic capacity to see apparitions.

In Chapter 7, I described Tegan, a child who entered my consultation room twelve months after she had 'died'. There is no question in my mind that I encountered her ethereal (light) form. I also believe that when Ralph was experiencing light, he was actually sensing his own ethereal body. The same, I feel, is true of others who see light during altered states of consciousness, such as in meditation, near-death experiences or following drugs. We all have an ethereal body, a subtle form in which the soul separates from the physical at 'death'. This subtle form is not in itself an angel. Whether or not it is angelic is determined by the quality of its consciousness.

When Ralph was dying he experienced liberation and lightness, with the sense that he was unlimited and able to bless everybody. The real 'blessing' that he gave was knowledge, as he seeded spiritual awareness in others. When Tegan entered my consultation room her presence created an atmosphere of light, love and healing. In effect those in the room received a 'blessing' of her company, and experienced the living truth of her spirit.

When Ralph was dying I said he was almost an angel. Although he experienced his subtle light form and had the freedom of a liberated mind, he was lacking in the power of realisation. His nature seemed angelic but the attainment was circumstantial and dependent on dying. As an attainment of human potential, the angel emerges from deep self-realisation and connection with the divine. By awakening to this potential before he died, I feel that Ralph *now* has the prospect of its full attainment and expression.

In Raja Yoga the angelic stage is considered the ultimate aim and object of meditation. Those who attain it can, at will, alternate with the seed stage discussed in the last chapter. The seed stage is a powerful transforming union in which all sense of personal involvement is lost, as the soul be-comes a channel for divine energy. The angelic stage is a more engaging union, where the soul becomes like God. One maintains a sense of self, whilst expressing divinity through spiritual knowledge, powers and virtues. With the angelic stage a soul attracts to itself but acts in the image of the divine. Surrendered and free from ego, it inspires others to seek and express their own angelic qualities.

The angelic stage is a likeness to God, revealed through those who have the courage to grow. Those that make effort to transform themselves will progressively attain this. Their sign is that they remain constantly carefree, light and beyond the limited concerns of this world. On account of purity they are welcomed everywhere as gentle and virtuous, giving courage and hope to souls 'lost' in a body-conscious world.

Such is the angelic stage of attainment.

Through truth, simplicity, awareness and realisation it is a human potential.

TWENTY-SEVEN

A Mission of Love

Elisabeth Kübler-Ross has stated that there are only three types of people in the world today who are honest: children, the dying and psychotics. The latter was a particularly interesting observation from a psychiatrist. In fact psychotic states are conditions I sometimes see in my work, and view with interest. I think that those who are psychotic, sometimes encounter their spiritual potential in a totally unbalanced way. We refer to this as having delusions of grandeur. Whilst out of touch with this world during a florid mental illness, they have no capacity to lie and relate only what they are feeling.

Early in my career as a palliative care physician I developed a close relationship with a young man who died of AIDS. Damon Courtenay's story has since become public following its publication in his father's book *April Fool's Day* (Penguin, Melbourne, 1998). When we first met he was twenty-two and had already suffered in his life. He was born with haemophilia, a bleeding disorder due to the deficiency of one clotting factor. Damon was frequently hospitalised during episodes of bleeding, for intravenous injections of the missing factor. One feature of the condition is spontaneous bleeding into joints. Apart from acute painful episodes, Damon developed crippling deformities in his joints, which affected his mobility. He walked with a limp and couldn't remember a day in his life that he hadn't suffered pain.

The timing of his illness was crucial to the following events. It was during the 1980s just before AIDS became apparent to the Western world. The clotting factors given to Damon had been unwittingly taken from AIDS-infected blood donors. When AIDS was discovered, and Damon was tested, he was found to be HIV-positive. Damon was one of those people who come through hardship with great character development. He was endearing, sharp and mischievous, with a totally positive outlook on life. He and his carer, Celeste, took to me when I determined that his chronic diarrhoea was unrelated to AIDS but had been induced by his pain-killers. Not only were we able to get rid of this long-standing problem but we also achieved better pain control than he had experienced in living memory.

Despite a 'roller-coaster' of problems over the next two years, Damon always had a smile and a new 'money-making scheme' when I saw him. Although he had significant periods of doubt and depression, I never saw him dejected and he never lost his love for life.

'Whenever things are difficult,' his father had said, 'there is a place you can go to.'

He enjoyed talking to me about spiritual matters. A gift from his childhood was something that his father had taught him. 'Whenever things are difficult,' his father had said, 'there is a place you can go to. A place that is always safe, and one where you are protected. It is a small quiet place, within you. Go there whenever you need to escape, or when you need to concentrate on something.' Damon learnt to access this place inside, and used it frequently throughout his childhood. What his father had inadvertently taught him, was how to meditate and how to be soul-conscious. This gift, I believe, would become the most valuable lesson of his relatively short life. He wasn't actually aware of it as enlightened, it was simply a natural practice. He could 'go beyond' his body and the ravages of disease at will.

During the progression of AIDS, Damon had a psychotic episode where he temporarily lost his sanity. One of the neuropsychiatric manifestations of AIDS is mania. This is a condition characterised by delusions of grandeur, paranoia and 'speedy' irrational thoughts and actions. Over a six-week period he became progressively more paranoid and irrational, convinced that the CIA was after him. It culminated in a hospital admission to an AIDS-unit that was poorly equipped to manage psychiatric ill-nesses. Damon suddenly became totally irrational and ran away from the hospital, terrified that *they* were coming to get him. A terrible scene followed in the family home.

Because he was considered insane he was scheduled (declared insane), and the police were sent after him. Despite his frail, weak and wasted condition, they forcibly arrested him in front of his shocked family and carers. Damon was taken screaming and terrified to a psychiatric hospital, where he had to be forcibly detained and medicated. This was in the early days of AIDS, when there was a huge amount of fear and misinformation about its mode of transmission. He was initially treated like a 'leper', though this subsequently worked in his favour, as he was assigned a house in the grounds with his own nursing staff. I went to see him a day after his admission.

The house was an old, musty weatherboard place with pleasant gardens. It was completely surrounded by a high fence, with a double-locked gate. I was shown to the facility by an orderly, who unlocked a huge padlock and removed the chain to let me in. As I walked towards the house, the chain rattled behind me as I was padlocked in with Damon and his 'keepers'. Damon was waiting for me on the veranda.

On recognising me he waved with a huge smile; evidently he was very, very happy.

Far from a prisoner, Damon greeted me like a 'lord of the manor', and proceeded to show me around his new kingdom. He introduced me to all the nurses on a first-name basis, telling me that they were his servants! He had no memory of his florid paranoia of the previous day, and none whatsoever of the traumatic events surrounding his detention. He told me that his AIDS had been cured by electromagnetic emissions from a small copper bracelet on his wrist. He said that very soon the whole world would be free from AIDS and all other diseases. As he, Damon, had discovered the secret of eternal life, he was now very important indeed. Consequently he had been given new headquarters in the hospital, and had been put in charge. The government would soon remove all the patients from the hospital to make room for his operation, which would change the world.

These were the essential themes that Damon related to me. He was excited and spoke quickly, going off on numerous tangents as he did. This creates what we term a 'word salad' of linked but dissociated themes. I have picked the main characters from the 'salad' to express where he was mainly 'coming from'. One of his tangents was a salad created on the word eternal. 'I know God has put me here for this purpose. He wants everyone to live forever. He has given me a mission. Yes, it's a mission, a mission of love. This is why I'm here. The only thing the world needs now, now that I can heal everyone, is to love. This is why the government has made me the boss around here. Eternal life means nothing without love. Giving people eternal life was only the first part, now I have to make them love. I'm a man on a mission.'

Damon was beaming with satisfaction. He was euphoric and absolutely intoxicated with his 'insights'. He was also floridly manic and psychotic. Some months later, when he'd finally recovered from his manic condition, he would confide in Celeste that he missed the certainty, the sense of invincibility, of his own strength in mind and body which the mania had given him. As Damon grew increasingly frail and incapable in the last year of his life, he would some-times say wistful things to her, 'It was so great, babe! It was the first time in my life I felt completely whole! I *was* the mighty Damon. If only I could be well and have that same feeling again.'

Despite his deterioration, he maintained his mission of love. In an excerpt from his diary, which was published in *April Fool's Day* two years after he died, he said this:

> … Can I tap into a force within my mind to beat the odds, to sur-vive? Love is the most powerful force of all. It is an energy, it is a power. I must use it constructively. I must *stop* listening to the neg-ative forces in my head that tell me that it is beginning to end. I want to give so much to this world, to the people I love.

Then, a little later he said this:

> … How to start? The first thing is to have faith in myself again. To take control. To get my brain working again. To live my life around a structured existence. Now I must read, I must write, I must con-tribute to the person that is me … I must learn to live again.

He concluded with the following words:

> … anything can be done if the will is strong enough. It is truly time to explore the spiritual nature of the person that is me. I use that word to describe that which is more than the heart, the bowel, the knee joint. That which makes us more than merely flesh and blood. For that is where the answer to healing and to thriving and to exis-tence and to life is to be found.

When he was dying in Celeste's arms, I believe Damon found himself to be that small, quiet 'place within' that his father had shown him. I think he discovered in that place the secret of eternal life. For that place was himself with all the illusions removed. And it was his mission realised, for that place was love. I feel the soul that was Damon has moved on to serve the world, and that his mission of love now has the wisdom of a short and full life.

In the last few chapters we have looked at expressions of soul-consciousness. These are states of attainment, in which one's eternal identity is realised and emerged, such that its purity and grace is visible to the world. They are also states in which the soul has the power to extend its consciousness beyond the physical body; and states in which the soul can act as a channel for love from the divine. Damon said that 'eternal life means nothing without love', and he stated that he was now on 'a mission of love'. To seek the spiritual path, to make effort to draw upon the perfection of that small, quiet 'place within', to find God, and to extend this awareness as a merciful unifying compassion for all life; this is the mission of love.

TWENTY-EIGHT

Love's Mission

After entering this world our innocence is progressively conditioned by body-consciousness. As the soul becomes body-conscious, it depends on vices to protect itself and to satisfy its desires. Acceptance of death reveals how a soul can rediscover its original nature of peace. Cathartic and near-death experiences show how enlightenment can lead to the path of realisation. Spiritual effort demonstrates that we can free ourselves from body-consciousness and rediscover our purity. Spiritual growth, then, is a paradoxical journey of 'remembering' who we were. As a journey to love, it can be summarised thus: *As I was, then so I shall become.*

In the midst of mania, Damon Courtenay told me that he was on a mission of love. He later wrote that love, as 'the most powerful force of all', must be used constructively. One of the mistakes of body-consciousness is that we seek love on the outside, when really it lies within. We try to use love and direct love, rather than become it. Our principal mistake is that we mix love with attachment until, fettered with need and dependency, it becomes conditional. We withhold it from those who misbehave, and feel unhappy or angry when it isn't reciprocated. On the one hand, we seek to direct and determine who is worthy of love while, on the other, we find we cannot trust it.

The love that lies latent within is that of our original soul-conscious nature. It is both pure and unconditional. Only when we are soul-conscious can we encounter what it is like to love unconditionally. This may happen before death, during enlightenment, following a catharsis or through spiritual practices. What you experience is simply that you become love itself. You are indivisible from it and so full and complete in its experience that you have no other desires. When I experienced unconditional love following a catharsis, it wasn't love for anybody or anything in my life. I simply was it. If I had said at the time, 'I am love', this would have accurately described my feeling of identity during the experience.

What I discovered about unconditional love is that it cannot be directed or controlled. You can be it but you can't give it. The moment you direct it to one person or withhold it from another, you have placed a condition on it. Ego and attachment intervene as you decide where it should go. As you become soul-conscious then unconditional love emanates from your original personality. The giving of love accords with its own nature rather than your direction. There is no need to help it in any way, for love has its own power. To love unconditionally we must detach from everything else and become love, then let love 'decide'.

If one becomes love then there is nothing to prove, for love is apparent and instantly recognisable.

A mission can be either a vocation or a place for spiritual service. For Damon Courtenay it was a vocation to bring insights of love and healing to the world. Those who countenance spirituality will entertain the vocation of serving humanity through love. However, because it is easy to mix ego with good intention, it is useful to consider the vocations that love itself has. We should ask ourselves: What is love's mission? This helps us to be humble and to have the humility to 'let go and let love'. If one becomes love then there is nothing to prove, for love is apparent and instantly recognisable. No force is required as love itself can accomplish its own task.

When someone is dying in acceptance they let go of everything and become love. Those who encounter such people recognise this and comment on its beauty. In Chapter 5, June told me of such an experience, which left her with a firm belief in eternal life. It was, she said, as if her mother became a 'mirror', reflecting back the truth of spirit to those who visited her. A number of the yogis I encountered in Mt Abu had this capacity in life. Their presence could give such an experience of love that all that remained was spiritual conviction. My own experience of post-cathartic love changed me from an atheist to a theist, and led me to a spiritual path.

Love's vocation reveals who we are, transforms body-conscious attitudes and illuminates the path of realisation. Its mission is to unify and heal the world. On a mission of love our task is to become love, then to allow *it* the freedom to accomplish its own purpose.

TWENTY-NINE

The Power of Love

In India the term for religion is dharma, which literally translated means 'way of life'. Religion as a way of life, is what we term spirituality in the West. Irrespective of our particular religion we can achieve spirituality in its expression. True religion, I feel, is the inculcation and expression of all the virtues. It aims not to convert but rather to enable others to experience and express their personal truth. No spiritual path is absolute, though I believe the divine to be an external guiding influence, which serves all religions. This service is through the power of love, which has within it unlimited healing potential.

Unconditional love is divine spiritual love. Not only is it latent within but it also resides externally in the divine. If we encounter it externally, the power of love reveals that which is latent within. If we encounter it internally, then love expands until we are indivisible from the divine.

Whatever we experience in life, whatever traumas we encounter and whatever defences we erect, love lies beyond that. However we have changed, however we have been tainted, love awaits our awakening to heal us of the past and free us in the present. At a meditation workshop a few years ago Monica, a teacher, took me aside to speak to me of a past trauma. When she was a child, her father molested her for a number of years, extending into her adolescence. She thought that she had dealt with its traumatic effects, until one of her students confided that she too had been through sexual abuse. In trying to help the student through bitterness, remorse and guilt she found her own pain resurfacing.

She was angry and bitter that she couldn't confront her father, who had since died. She was also angry with her mother, who had been weak and ineffectual after she discovered the abuse. So disturbing were the memories that they were affecting her marriage and capacity to work. She was also struggling with a dilemma of how to confront her now frail and aged mother. After developing panic attacks and insomnia, she had recently consulted a psychotherapist. Monica said that she felt the experience had left her soul filthy and eternally tainted. She asked me what I thought.

After acknowledging her pain, I talked to her about the soul, of its original purity and how it is conditioned by what we experience. When we are traumatised we find ways of repressing our pain. We lay protective layers like onion rings around the soul, and learn to express ourselves in ways that keep us from being vulnerable.

'It is impossible for the soul to be eternally blighted through traumas or life-experience.'

Although we hide the pain, such that we don't feel it, it still resides within and can reawaken. I said that deeper than this, beneath the 'onion rings', lies our original purity and innocence. As with the repression of emotional pain it too has been forgotten and can reawaken.

'Nothing that ever touches you can harm this,' I said. 'It is impossible for the soul to be eternally blighted through traumas or life-experience.' I went on to say that I hoped she would experience this deepest part of herself during the week-end workshop. I felt that it would then be unnecessary for her to confront her elderly mother about things that had happened so long ago.

Monica wrote to me after the weekend. On the afternoon of the second day she had an experience of profound love and healing, which brought a sense of cleanliness and release. In reflecting upon her experience, she said it felt like a complete purification through the power of love. Recognising this love to be intrinsic, she was no longer influenced by her childhood, had forgiven her father and felt no need to discuss it with her mother.

On my second visit to India in 1998, I went to Mt Abu with the aim of discovering how to realise this power of love consistently. At dawn on the fourth day I left the main group and walked to a nearby valley for meditation. The setting was one of perfect beauty, solitude and silence except for morning birdsong. As I meditated I held a conversation with God in my mind. I said, 'I renounce all my attachments to this world and surrender to you alone. I let go of my body, my relationships, my physical wealth and possessions, and even the sense of who I am.' I finished by repeating over and over, 'I surrender to you alone.' As I did so, I experienced myself becoming a direct child of God, which gave me a feeling of belonging to the divine. Through the relationship of a child, I also had the feeling that God belonged to me. With this experience of belonging I had an encounter with love, which I can only describe as purity and power. Neither a feeling nor an emotion, it was an intelligent life-transforming energy.

'... I experienced the power of love as a purifying energy.'

Like Monica, I experienced the power of love as a purifying energy. We can experience its healing qualities under many circumstances, whilst living or dying. I believe its source to be the divine, and that its awakening comes through surrender and belonging. I feel that love teaches through the power of realisation and makes us like the divine. More accurately, I believe that pure love reaches us to reawaken the image of God that 'sleeps' within us. I think that it would please God if we were to become like Him/Her. I think that this is how we return the love of the divine.

THIRTY

Merciful Vision

The power of love is experienced when we become receptive to it through right thoughts, right words and right actions. Beyond this, to extend the healing power of love to the world, we must have no tension or conflict with anything in it. Merciful vision is an attitude which eliminates all division and unifies one's capacity for love with others.

The plea of Jesus at the crucifixion, 'Forgive them Father, for they know not what they do,' is a simple yet complete expression of mercy. Body-consciousness is a 'blindfold' that separates us from love and truth. It deceives us. Under its influence, fear and mistrust distort perception until the soul no longer acts according to its virtues. In time we come to 'know not what we do'. Spiritual insight makes us aware that this is the basis for human weakness. Within this knowledge lies understanding, acceptance and forgiveness.

Imagine that a small child comes into your lounge, leans on an expensive vase and accidentally smashes it on the floor. The child doesn't know what a vase is, and has no sense of its value. As the child had no idea that the vase could move, let alone fall over, you would consider he or she blameless and innocent. Even though there is loss, you would not have to forgive because you understand that the child lacks knowledge and experience.

Likewise, people who have become body-conscious have 'forgotten' truth. As they act without knowledge or experience of the soul, they separate themselves from love. Merciful vision is an attitude of true forgiveness, which accepts everyone as blameless and innocent. It allows love and its mission to propagate and spread through society. To develop merciful vision requires faith in our immortality, trust in the divine and acceptance of the unfolding drama. We must also have a lot of love for our human family. Rather than seeing our differences in gender, race, attitudes and behaviour, we can develop a unifying sense of brotherhood (or sisterhood). By considering all souls to be children of God, we develop the feeling of a family where everyone belongs to one-another. In soul-consciousness we realise the power of love through belonging to the divine. Merciful vision brings a sense of belonging to the world, which connects this power of love to other souls.

Merciful vision is an attitude of true forgiveness, which accepts everyone as blameless and innocent.

In the teachings of Raja Yoga there is a slogan, '*When you change, the world changes*', which reflects two things. First, as we become soul-conscious, we see and experience the world differently, so the world changes for us. Second, we begin to cooperate with love's task of revealing truth, creating unity and healing the world. As we play our part, as we cooperate with love, our merciful vision is more than a way of seeing the world, it is a way of allowing love into it.

THIRTY-ONE

Realisation as a Cycle

A s we 'grow' and realise our original nature of peace, purity and power, we embody love. In this return to love, we complete a cycle from soul-consciousness to body-consciousness and back again. Realisation, I believe, is part of the life cycle of every human soul. We each fall from grace, some further than others do, but our hidden purity cannot be subdued forever. We are responsible for our actions and have to settle our accounts, but love is latent and ultimately irrepressible.

I believe in birth, death and rebirth, and feel that life is a drama in which all souls play a part on the world stage. New souls enter this drama, while old souls continue to be reborn into a growing civilisation. When we fall from grace so too does our growing civilisation, as its values come to reflect increasing body-consciousness. Realisation in the individual often follows a crisis, which challenges or destroys the facades of body-consciousness. In its broadest application to humanity, cyclical realisation might see a crisis reached wherein civilisations rise and fall, self-destruct and renew. If this is true, then we could expect a scene in 'the drama' where the world transforms in the midst of chaos.

I received one such warning in 1987 from Vincent, a terminally-ill AIDS patient. At thirty-seven he had suffered from the illness for two years and had advanced Kaposi's sarcoma, a malignant condition characterised by purple patches growing in the skin. By the time I met Vincent, this had also spread to his liver, lungs and spleen. He had been in the hospice for three weeks when he asked me to pay him a special visit. As he had no medical or psychiatric disturbance of the mind, what he had to say was intriguing.

He told me that he had been having visions of the future. In these he saw two main features that foretold of impending cataclysm. On one side he saw a nuclear world war, causing mass destruction of human life. On the other, a series of natural disasters culminating in huge earthquakes, tidal waves and flooding. He said these events would occur at around the turn of the century. 'The first sign,' he said, 'is a tyrant, worse than Hitler, who would emerge from the East.'

He said that the events all had spiritual significance and that these were 'biblical times'. Armageddon, he told me, was not the clash of good and evil depicted in the Old Testament. It was a 'nuclear cleansing' for mankind. Likewise the apocalyptic scenes of natural disasters were to prepare the world for revelation, and the coming of a new age. In these final scenes of his vision he saw a legion of angels bringing love, unity and healing to the world in its darkest hour.

Vincent said, 'Dr Cole, I haven't told anyone else of these things.' Pointing upwards he said, 'I was "instructed" to tell you because, in time, you would understand. I guess you'll probably think I'm crazy but I had to tell you.' His final words were given with emphasis. I thanked Vincent and assured him that I didn't think of him as crazy, although I was more of a sceptic in those days.

Despite his vision, Vincent didn't have a particularly peaceful death. He had been depressed before the hospice admission and struggled within himself, right up to dying three weeks after our discussion. He never spoke to me again of visions; in fact he became quite 'distanced', with-drawn and troubled. At the end he became breathless and agitated with pneumonia but was able to die comfortably under sedation.

Vincent's predictions accord with those of other vision-aries and psychic commentators for this millennium. Best known is Nostradamus, a naturopath and astrologer of the Renaissance period. The fame and influence of his lifetime, stemmed from the accuracy of his predictions, which brought him into circles of 'high society'. The problem with prophesy, however, is that it only becomes objective after the fact. Nostradamus' predictions have been given credi-bility due to a remarkable accuracy in relating to some events of this century. Nevertheless, the prophesy of cata-clysm could not be entertained without widespread scepti-cism, until after it has happened. This in turn would make it unpreventable! So prophesy has major limitations, and is not particularly useful to the wider community as a learn-ing or education tool.

Though sceptical, I didn't discard Vincent's warnings as I had been having similar, albeit less visionary meditation experiences. The encounter with Vincent occurred three years after I was enlightened by Kübler-Ross. It was over these years that I began to meditate on the divine nature and form of God. Instead of trying to reach the divine on my terms, I had recently discovered the experience to be easier when I simply 'allowed God'. There was no need for force. The divine is ever-present and all we need to do is to become open and accessible. By surrendering and 'allow-ing' God, I was learning to subjugate my ego to God's will. As a result, I began to experience a loving divine union, which included a compassionate feeling for humanity. I also began to receive impressions, not visions, of the times we live in. What I experienced in meditation was spirituality and truth emerging at a time of social decay. I sensed a divine community being established amidst scenes in which chaos, conflict and desperation preceded a global realisation and peace. There was, concurrently, world renewal and destruction of body-consciousness.

If realisation were a cyclical phenomenon then an enticing possibility exists, where prophecy could come from a 'memory' or sanskara within the soul. Having lived this age repeatedly, could Nostradamus, perhaps, have 'remembered' the future? If realisation is a cyclical phenomenon, we might expect to find cultural evidence for cyclical time. We might also expect to find evidence that technologically advanced civilisations have previously existed. Furthermore, if this is the age of realisation, it should be evident now that humanity is capable of self-destruction.

What I experienced in meditation was spirituality and truth emerging at a time of social decay.

In *Wisdom of the Elders* (Stoddart, Toronto, 1992), acclaimed scientist, author and 'environmentalist' David Suzuki contrasts Western science with the diametrically opposed traditions of 'age-old wisdom' from indigenous peoples around the world. Written with Peter Knudtson, the book explores the delicate relationship between humans, nature and the environment. Their research took accounts from surviving cultures within developed countries (American Indians, Australian Aboriginal people), as well as from third world communities.

They write that in the Western worldview, time which is linear and arrow-like underlies 'our most cherished notions of progress — our collective faith in the inexorable, incremental refinement of human society, technology and thought. Linear time … neatly aligns the jumble of past human experience that might otherwise seem unsettling or devoid of meaning into an orderly, chronological procession of sequential events, each officially assigned its own measure of importance.'

Native societies, by contrast, have traditionally embraced manifestations of circular time in the universe, 'sanctifying them with their rituals and awe'. Looking at the universe through the Western worldview, Suzuki and Knudtson say, one is fortunate to grasp even a transient sense of the spiritual rhythm and cycles of nature. Through the native eye, of cyclical time, nature is absorbed into a timeless dimension that is both spiritually and ecologically charged. The indigenous peoples of the world have respect for the land, its flora and fauna. They also have knowledge that to interfere with the cycles of nature is to invite destruction. Native worldview conveys that: '... familiar patterns of the past — great cycles of growth and decline, birth and death, ecological devastation and renewal — can, and perhaps will, re-emerge.'

... one is fortunate to grasp even a transient sense of the spiritual rhythm and cycles of nature.

An example given in their book is of the Navajo men and women from the southwestern USA. Cyclical time appears in their traditional stories of long-term expansions and contractions of the universe. They conceive that the world first stretches outward from the centre then springs back, culminating in a perfectly symmetrical, pulsating movement over the whole period. Cyclical time is also revealed in the creation stories of their ancestral holy people. These relate that the first people emerged from sacred openings to the core of the nurturing earth. They then dispersed across the land in all directions. In the great mythic cycle, the souls of deceased Navajo continuously return, and join with newborn souls to grant order to the natural world.

Many Navajo now believe that humankind is living quite precariously. The white man's attitude has destroyed the sacred and natural rhythms of nature, and a crucial time is coming — 'within a number of human generations' — where the earth and all its inhabitants will experience *another* period of cataclysmic collapse.

Such is also the widespread view of many different native peoples from around the planet. The difference between these beliefs and the prophesies we discussed earlier, is that they are based on mythology, rather than psychic phenomena. As we shall see, there is evidence that mythology has a sound factual base, handed down in story-form through successive generations.

Graham Hancock explores this in a compelling book, *Fingerprints of the Gods* (Crown, New York, 1995). He compiles evidence that past civilisations existed, which were both sophisticated and more technologically advanced than we are today. In a journey through Central and South America and the Middle East, he catalogues and details the unexplained mysteries of these regions. He also identifies common threads in the mythological beliefs of ancient, now extinct, peoples that were geographically and culturally distinct.

Mythologies from both the Middle East and the Americas have a 'Noah's Ark' scenario, which is caste in images of cataclysm, destruction and flooding, followed by widespread community disorder. In the Americas, 'civilisers' are then depicted to have come into those communities, bringing order and high-living values. Pictures, carvings and statues depict these as bearded Caucasians in white robes, despite the fact that the communities they entered were of non-Caucasian background. They were also depicted as leaving again by sea in an age when we were, supposedly, unable to navigate let alone have the technology to travel across the Atlantic.

Hancock concluded that the whole developed world was flooded at an apocalyptic time of massive earthquakes and volcanic activity; that the society of the time was both sophisticated and technologically advanced; and that the cataclysm wiped out most of the population. The existence of common themes, within culturally distinct groups, suggests that there is a factual basis to what is generally considered myth. It also appears that those communities recorded, and handed down, their stories to successive generations. That 'Noah's Ark' occurred in the Middle East and the Americas, suggests that a common experience founded these stories.

He gives further evidence that flooding and a raised sea level affected a developed civilisation in Lake Titicaca. Once a seaport community with elaborate farming and irrigation techniques, Lake Titicaca is now 3820 metres above sea level. Their sophisticated techniques are now being studied for modern-day application. Building techniques used in Machu Pichu in Peru, as well as the pyramids in Egypt and Mexico, still defy explanation. Huge stones with smoothly cut surfaces that we cannot yet replicate, are aligned with pristine accuracy. There are only a handful of cranes capable of lifting these today and none that could have aligned them at the locations they are in. Apart from size and alignment, the mathematical technology used for the planning processes is only now emerging with modern computing techniques.

A fascinating mystery surrounds cartography, or mapping, of our oceans. The land mass of Antarctica is accurately outlined on maps dating back as far as AD 1513 (the Piri Reis Map, made at Constantinople). Yet it is known that this coastline had been covered in ice for thousands of years before that. The technology to identify a land mass under the ice has only been developed in the latter half of the twentieth century, and it has confirmed that maps drawn centuries ago were accurate. Thus, as it is known that the Antarctic coastline couldn't have been drawn in our recorded history, Hancock concludes that it must have been copied and handed down from originals drawn thousands of years ago. He also concludes that advanced technology must have been available at that time. He states that, as cartography is an activity of sophisticated communities, they must have been both civilised and well developed.

There is evidence, therefore, that advanced civilisations may have existed in the past, with access to some technologies we can't yet match. We now have the nuclear capacity to destroy our current civilisation. We have almost denuded the planet's natural forests, have created a hole in the ozone layer and appear unable to control our greenhouse gas emissions. Consequently, the world's weather patterns are changing, on the one hand with droughts and crop failures, on the other with massive flooding and other extremes. It seems to me that humankind has developed a huge karmic debt with the planet, which is being settled by nature itself.

Whatever upheavals you may witness in the world, uphold your eternal identity and allow the power of love to support souls during increasing difficulties.

In considering these possibilities, I would like to convey the possibility of a spiritual renewal emerging in a time of entropy and chaos. Whatever upheavals you may witness in the world, uphold your eternal identity and allow the power of love to support souls during increasing difficulties. In potentially difficult times ahead, let any disturbing scene invoke your spiritual efforts to bring peace to the world. Instead of getting caught up in the events, let yourself become of service through spiritual knowledge, love and understanding.

THIRTY-TWO

Through the Ashram of your Life

I was seated on my suitcase in Ahmadabad airport, on my return journey from India in 1992. There was nowhere else to sit. The domestic departure lounge was chaotic, my flight to Delhi being one of several that had been delayed. A group of angry Indian businessmen were shouting and gesticulating at the baggage handlers. Despite the disturbance, and despite being tightly scheduled for a connecting flight in Delhi, I felt blissfully detached and serene. 'Sweet drama!' I thought, and smiled inwardly. 'At least I have a seat.' Which was my suitcase.

I was enjoying a sensation of perfect inner peace, upheld against upheaval and chaos. I was not worried about making my connection in Delhi. I just observed everything without desire, concern or anxiety. I felt wonderfully free and liberated.

Any doubts that filtered through my mind during the meditation retreat in Mt Abu were dispelled. At that moment it seemed as if they were dispelled forever. In fact they had dispersed on 'Baba's Rock', in the afterglow of a magnificent sunset meditation. High in the mountains of Abu, the divine had 'spoken' to me in a 'voice' that still echoed through my mind. It was a secret whisper of how to commune in His/Her divine nature. *'Through the "ashram" of your life,'* it had said.

At the end of the meditation retreat I had nothing planned for the following week. I had heard from visiting Western Raja Yogis, that a special meeting was to take place. A meeting in which the divine supposedly communicates and gives directions based on the soul and the cycle of realisation. I was urged to stay but there were a few things that I didn't know about. Those who could attend this meeting are allowed to be there on the basis of their spiritual effort, self-knowledge and surrender. They also had to have followed certain disciplines of purity for a number of months.

I was enjoying a sensation of perfect inner peace, upheld against upheaval and chaos.

To stay on I needed permission from Dadi Janki, a head-administrator of the organisation. Physically short in stature, she had disarming power in her spirituality. She engaged me with a sensitive challenge to my spiritual commitment. If I accepted this knowledge, surrendered myself, and adopted the disciplines of pure living then I could stay. If not, then they would be unable to accommodate me. I was to go away and think about this, then return to see her again in a couple of days.

I had expected to know clearly, one way or the other, what to do. As it turned out, I was left with considerably more uncertainty than I had before meeting her. No longer was it just about staying, it now had another unexpected dimension. Was I spiritual enough? My feelings fluctuated between indignation and self-doubt over the next few days. If such an opportunity exists how can one person deny another such a meeting. Beneath this was a nagging feeling of being unworthy.

In the midst of these feelings I found myself attracted to the communal life of these yogis. I was drawn towards surrendering myself and living the 'monastic' lifestyle of the ashram. (Ashram is an Eastern term that describes a spiritual community following common principles and teachings.) So further confusion compounded my doubts and uncertainty: Should I leave my life for this? Will I find God in this place? Do I surrender and stay here? Is this attraction part of the divine plan for me?

The answers came, not through a meeting the following week, but later that very same day on 'Baba's Rock', Mt Abu's favourite place for sunset meditations. As the sun disappeared that evening, my awareness was beyond all its beauty. There were no physical sensations, as my body, the earth and the universe seemed to stand still. It felt like I was in a time warp, filled with divine insight, and unaware, temporarily, of my own existence.

I cannot say that it was an experience of love; that would follow. Nor can I say that it was an experience of peace; that also would follow. What I can say is this. It was an experience of clarity and of divine presence, and of a voice speaking in the deepest, most ancient part of my soul. Its words of wisdom and direction finished all my confusion about divine meetings and finding God. It said, '*It is not by life in an ashram, that you will find Me. But it is through the ashram of your life, that you will know Me.*'

As you develop and experience the reality of your spiritual beliefs, they become a power in your life and lead to the natural expression of inner beauty, wisdom and strength.

The message was a dual one of example and service. As you develop and experience the reality of your spiritual beliefs, they become a power in your life and lead to the natural expression of inner beauty, wisdom and strength. Observing without judgement, you reveal love. Speaking without arrogance, you teach love. Acting without complexity, you become love. When you become love, you belong to the divine and your life becomes the ashram.

It also becomes a mission.

THIRTY-THREE

Simplicity

*T*he habits of body-consciousness make spiritual growth and attainment seem esoteric, elaborate and challenging. Yet the original nature of the soul was one of great simplicity. Complexity arises when body-consciousness conditions the soul, with its dependencies, desires and uncertainties. It is actually body-consciousness, rather than spiritual attainment and realisation, that is complex. What we are seeking is simplicity and truth.

If you exclude the body what remains is thought energy, an organising intellect and memories (including sanskaras). We are all the same whatever our gender, beliefs or cultural background. If we leave the current life we do so as this living energy, which is consciousness. In transforming body-consciousness and realising our true nature we are becoming sensible. We can look at the same world and be deceived through body-conscious eyes, yet understand it accurately when we are soul-conscious.

Raja Yoga teaches that consciousness emanates from a point of light, which is the form of the soul. Although the form never changes its simplicity, purity and power do. In Raja Yoga, God is considered the only soul who never enters the cycle of birth and death. Without gender, He or She never becomes body-conscious and never loses His or Her purity and power. With such simplicity, the Supreme Soul never seeks to direct or control love and never becomes attached to anything. As God remains eternally in His or Her original nature, He or She never stops being love and never stops allowing love. In time, all souls can rediscover their original peace, purity and power through this one who never changes.

When we are body-conscious the soul seems esoteric, yet it is our true identity. We substitute the new reality of that which we deem objective, measurable, concrete. We turn away from truth and instead embrace the temporary illusion of body-consciousness. The mysterious, the unexplainable or the miraculous amaze us, yet these are ordinary expressions of our original nature. Soul-consciousness heals us of ignorance and deception, yet we think of this as enlightenment. To grow back to who we were, to return to love, we need to understand that soul-consciousness is our most ordinary, uncomplicated way of being.

In time, all souls can rediscover their original peace, purity and power through this one who never changes.

With soul-conscious simplicity we are easy, open and honest. In simplicity, truth is visible and realised with nothing to prove. Through it we experience the depth of our own truth, become economical with our lives, and benevolent with our love.

There is nothing elaborate about soul-consciousness. As you journey through these paradoxes, your influence will grow, as you become more ordinary. There is no need to change anyone but yourself. Love will do the rest.

Have a good life and a good journey.
Be simple, be you.
Be sensible, be true.

Om shanti.

A Note on the
Brahma Kumaris

The Brahma Kumaris World Spiritual University is an international organisation, which teaches Raja Yoga meditation as a free community service. It is affiliated with the United Nations as a non-government organisation with consultative status in the Economic and Social Council, and with consultative status in UNISEF.

Should you wish to look further into the meditation philosophy discussed here, I have listed the contact numbers of the main centres in Australia and throughout the world. From these contacts you can obtain the details of centres or contacts near you, and determine whether there are courses available in your area if you live at some distance from the main centres. All teaching is voluntary and most centres run a free four-week introductory course in meditation. As these contact details are subject to change, you may prefer to access the Brahma Kumaris Internet site at <www.bkwsu.com> for a current listing of international contact numbers, or more information about the organisation.

Brahma Kumaris Main Centres

Australia
Australian Capital Territory
  Canberra — (02) 6260 5525

New South Wales
  Ashfield (Sydney) — (02) 9716 7066
  Newcastle — (02) 4942 4060
  North Ryde (Sydney) — (02) 9805 1251
  Wollongong — (02) 4285 0889 or (02) 4226 9661

Queensland
  Gold Coast—(07) 5572 9888
  Milton (Brisbane)—(07) 3368 2391

South Australia
  Adelaide — (08) 8269 7811

Tasmania
  Hobart — (03) 6223 5460

Victoria
  Baxter (Retreat Centre) — (03) 5971 1599
  Caulfield (Melbourne) — (03) 9528 4995
  Fitzroy (Melbourne) — (03) 9417 4883
  Geelong — (03) 5222 2241
  North Balwyn (Melbourne) — (03) 9857 8871

Western Australia
  Fremantle — (08) 9336 3396

Canada
  Toronto — +1 416 537 3034

China
  Hong Kong — +852 2806 3008

Fiji
  Suva — +679 307 799

Ireland
Dublin — +353 1 6603 967

Malaysia
Kuala Lumpur — +60 3 282 6396

New Zealand
Auckland — +64 9 579 5646
Christchurch — +64 3 389 7978
Dunedin — +64 3 473 7137
Napier — +64 6 835 8956
Wellington — +64 4 567 0699

Philippines
Manila — +63 2 890 7960

Singapore
Singapore — +65 467 1742

United Kingdom
Cardiff — +44 1222 480557
Glasgow — +44 141 423 5141
Jersey — +44 1534 31522
London — +44 181 727 3350

United States of America
New York — +1 516 773 0971